SOUTHERN
BRANCH LINES

A branch line reincarnated - two veteran AIX class 0-6-0Ts work on the Bluebell near Freshfield. The leading engine is the Stroudley liveried *Stepney* of 1875 assisting the 1872 built *Fenchurch*. The line, closed by BR in March 1958, was to reopen again in August 1960 as the first standard gauge preserved passenger line in the country.

As part of our ongoing market research, we are always pleased to receive comments about our books, suggestions for new titles, or requests for catalogues. Please write to: The Editorial Director, Oxford Publishing Co., Sparkford, Near Yeovil, Somerset, BA22 7JJ

SOUTHERN
BRANCH LINES

C. J. Gammell

Oxford Publishing Co.

The station booking hall of the sixties was little changed since the building of the railway. The timber structure of the South Eastern Railway at Elmers End, junction for two branch lines, is seen here in BR days, on 22 March 1969. The floor has been sprinkled with water and disinfectant and swept, whilst around the walls are the standard notices of the time including the 'fog service', a reduced service that operated at short notice in the era of the great fogs of the fifties and sixties. The diminutive bookstall has its own gas supply, the station being entirely gas lit. The entrance door to the platform has no handle. This door would be locked as the train departed to prevent accidents to latecomers who would otherwise rush from the booking hall at the last moment.

BR (SR)

© C. J. Gammell 1997

First Published in 1997

A catalogue record for this book is available from the British Library.

ISBN 0 86093 537 X

Oxford Publishing Co. is an imprint of Haynes Publishing, Sparkford, Nr Yeovil, Somerset BA22 7JJ

Printed in Hong Kong

Typeset in Times Roman Medium

Contents

Cowes station in March 1957 shows parcels being loaded into an LBSCR coach. The board by the station name was used as a ramp to get heavy parcels into the guard's brake. At the rear of the station is a noticeboard with handbills tied on with string advertising various excursions on the island.

Preface

The Southern Railway 1923 to 1947, and its successor the Southern Region of British Railways, was one of the most remarkable railway systems ever to exist. The railway systems in Britain had been grouped in 1923 to form four large railways, and the Southern, by way of its geographical location, was the odd one out. The three other railways carried the nation's freight, connected the principal cities of the country with the Capital and served the industrial heartland of the Midlands, the North and Wales. The Southern was a passenger-carrying railway but had an enormous variety of traffic. There were international trains to the Continent, elegant Pullman services, and boat trains to and from Britain's premier passenger port at Southampton.

The Southern had the world's largest suburban electrified system and electrification was a policy that the management pursued with the utmost vigour. Over the electrified network, steam trains to the outer reaches of the railway intermingled with fast electric expresses. Southern locomotives were built for power and rapid acceleration – for this very reason the railway built the sturdy Maunsell designs and the unique Bulleid Pacifics. It was to the Southern that the LMS came for a powerful express locomotive design when Derby were incapable of building one, and it was North British who supplied them off the peg. Today, Maunsell engines are still at work – a testimony to the soundness of the design.

The Southern had a well organised engineering department which produced all the necessary buildings required from a catalogue of standardised parts, from a lamp-post to a complete station. The ballast was provided for the entire system from one railway owned quarry in the West of England. The railway never threw anything away, and redundant locomotives and rolling stock from electrified lines were transferred to other parts of the system. The Isle of Wight flourished on London & South Western Railway engines and South Eastern & Chatham, and London, Brighton & South Coast coaches.

The Southern, apart from creating its own image of green and white notices and nameboards, green coaches, engines and stations, had an extremely energetic publicity department. Every stone was turned to create more business, be it rambling in the Surrey Hills or gliding down to Bournemouth in the 'Belle'.

The three principal constituents, the LBSCR, SECR and LSWR, all had glorious histories to add to the Southern; and the Southern could boast, as part of the system, the world's first public railway (the Surrey Iron of 1804) and the first inter-city (Canterbury & Whitstable) built six months before the Liverpool & Manchester. The branch lines of the Southern reflected the history of the original owners, and no two branch lines were alike.

In the South East, ancient locomotives and rolling stock contrasted with modern multiple units, and the area became the stamping ground of Colonel Stephens and his activities. On the old 'Brighton' system superb Victorian architecture played host to ancient Stroudley engines, whilst in the West every line had a different class of locomotive. Hayling Island used AIXs exclusively until 1963, the Lyme Regis branch used Adams 4-4-2s and Wadebridge kept three elderly Beattie well tanks of 1874 for the Wenford Bridge line.

Today many of the branch lines in the country areas have gone for ever, but some have been preserved and preservation is growing. It is still possible to ride behind a 120-year-old engine in Sussex and listen to the distinctive beat of the Westinghouse air pump on the Isle of Wight. Many solid Victorian structures have survived to remind us of the railway's past.

Sheffield Park station in BR days.

Preface to the Second Edition

The Southern Railway and Southern Region are no longer in being and even the monolithic British Railways has disappeared. Great changes have taken place since the publication of the first edition in 1986 and a de-grouping of the railways has taken place which would have astonished even the astutest of railway observers ten years ago. A new structure of the country's railways has meant the creation of new companies. New preserved railways have come into being and the Channel Tunnel is now open. In London a new tram system is about to be built over existing branch lines and in Sussex, the Bluebell has been extended. The old Colonel Stephens' lines are being revived as the Kent & East Sussex has been extended and the East Kent reopened. The first section of the Spa Valley came into operation in December 1996 at Tunbridge Wells, the line to Eridge having closed in 1985. The Lavender Line continues to thrive under new ownership. The Isle of Wight Steam Railway has been extended to a new junction station at Smallbrook and the Swanage Railway now runs to Corfe Castle and beyond.

In Devon, the Lynton & Barnstaple Railway is reawakening and in Cornwall the Launceston Steam Railway has been extended while the Bodmin & Wenford Railway has reached Boscarne Junction. More footpaths and cycleways have been created over closed lines and a walk or ride along an old railway track has now become a way of life for the more energetic. Fewer lines are being closed nowadays and the country's politicians are becoming aware of the pollution problem. Railways still have a future and the growth of the Channel Tunnel traffic will promote more railway building in the former Southern area. The future at present looks bright, and one ponders over the wisdom of line closures in the 1960s for purely economic reasons.

C. J. Gammell,
London,
1997

The Southern halt had many standard features, and all components were made to a specification from a catalogue; the parts being produced at the Southern engineers' works at Exmouth Junction. The platform sections, fencing and nameboard parts could be seen throughout the system. Yarde Halt on the Torrington to Halwill line was only one coach length long and was opened on 27 July 1925.

Lens of Sutton

Branch Lines in South London

Bricklayers Arms

Bricklayers Arms, known to most railway staff as the 'Brick', was not so much a branch line as the end of the main line as the South Eastern Railway envisaged it. This short, 1¾-mile, line was opened to passengers on 1 May 1844 and gave the SER and the London & Croydon Railway independent access to London without having to pay the swingeing tolls charged by the London & Greenwich Railway over whose tracks the SER and L&CR had to ply to get into London Bridge. The South Eastern claimed Bricklayers Arms to be 'A Grand West End Terminal' but unfortunately, the London & Greenwich reduced the toll so that travel to London Bridge became less expensive. Passengers for the lucrative parts of West End, London were none too pleased with being dumped in the Old Kent Road and told to get a cab. Passenger operations ceased by 1852 and thereafter the branch was only used by specials for royalty and other dignitaries until the 1914-1918 war when the line was used for troop transportation. The Southern Railway revived the passenger service for excursions from 1932 until 1939.

In its early days the line was used by several royals including Queen Victoria on her way to Tunbridge Wells in 1849, her eldest daughter, Victoria, on her departure to Germany in 1858, and The Prince of Wales (King Edward VII) in March 1863. Bricklayers Arms is best known for the locomotive depot and the huge goods warehouses and sorting sidings. These all received a great deal of attention during the Second World War when the branch was bombed by the Luftwaffe on several occasions. Most of the warehouses were gutted and the loco shed damaged. The steam shed was the largest on the SER and its principal London depot. Bricklayers Arms' men had a wide route knowledge and worked to most parts of the system. The loco shed closed in 1962 after the electrification of the South Eastern Division and the last steam locomotive to traverse the branch was probably in 1966 when a Nine Elms 'Merchant Navy' was sent round to the workshops for wheel turning.

The branch closed to all traffic on 7 October 1983. The connection from North Kent West to North Kent East having closed on 20 June 1981 with the cessation of the parcels traffic. The line has since been sold off for industrial and housing development.

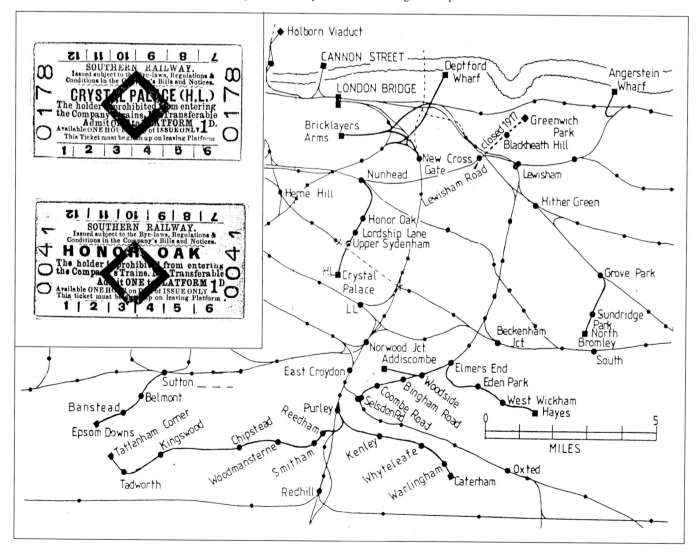

Deptford Wharf North signal box as seen in 1958 on the occasion of a visit by an RCTS railtour. The signal box had some of the original instruments including a repeater dated 1849. Note the bell on the roof and the double folding gates which crossed six tracks and had to be two-man operated. The site has been built over and little remains to be seen today.

Deptford Wharf

This short line of 1½ miles, from New Cross Gate and Old Kent Road Junction (1865) was opened in 1849 by the London, Brighton & South Coast Railway. The line never had a passenger service but was visited on 29 March 1958 and 3 October 1959 by the Railway Correspondence & Travel Society (RCTS) with a special push-and-pull railmotor set and an H class 0-4-4 tank. The wharf was used for importing coal and timber which was transhipped from barges. The coal went to Waddon Marsh and to the rest of the LBSCR system. In the May 1948 the branch was worked by LBSCR E6 class 0-6-2Ts, the crews being supplied by Bricklayers Arms' men, formerly of New Cross Gate. The line closed to freight on 15 October 1963 and little can be seen today as most of the area has been built upon. In an article in the July 1973 issue of *Railway World*, W. G. Rugman refers to the Grove Street crossing gates worked from the signal box. The gates had to cover six tracks and must have been one of the longest pairs in existence, so long in fact that it took two men in windy conditions to push them open! Deptford Wharf also had the Grove Street tramway connected to it and this was worked by the Wharf shunter through the streets, similar to Weymouth Quay.

Angerstein Wharf

This ¾-mile, freight only branch was built privately by Mr Angerstein who leased it to the SER. The line opened in 1852 and is still in use, the principal traffic being sea dredged ballast landed for Marcon and loaded into 100-ton wagons. Only two known passenger trains have traversed the line –

these were two railtours organised by the RCTS on 29 March 1958 and 3 October 1959.

Greenwich Park

The London, Chatham & Dover Railway opened its line to Greenwich Park on 1 October 1888 but it ceased to be of much use after the 1899 amlgamation as it duplicated the more direct South Eastern line. On 1 January 1917 the SECR closed the Greenwich Park branch along with other lines and stations as part of the economies enforced on most railway companies to save manpower, locomotives and rolling stock. Many inner suburban stations were never to reopen but the Greenwich Park branch survived in part. On completion of the Lewisham loops on 7 July 1929, freight and passenger trains used the former Greenwich Park branch from Lewisham to Nunhead where the line connected with the Catford Loop. An interesting survival of the Greenwich Park branch is the station building in Lewisham Road: although closed in 1917, the station building is complete. Inside can be seen the booking office with ticket office window and waiting rooms. The building is currently in use as a furniture sale room. The Ibis Hotel now occupies the Greenwich Park station site.

Crystal Palace (High Level)

The LBSCR had already got to Crystal Palace in 1854 with a short branch from the main line at Sydenham. At the close of the Great Exhibition in London's Hyde Park on 11 October 1851, over 6 million people had visited the site. Public interest was so great that a company was formed to re-erect the building on Sydenham Hill. Leo Schuster, a director of the

Greenwich Park was a terminus of the former London, Chatham & Dover Railway which was opened in 1888 but was closed on 1 January 1917. The site was derelict for many years and was a car park until the Orbis Hotel was built in the town centre.

Lens of Sutton

LBSCR, sold his estate of 300 acres to the Crystal Palace Company, and the chairman of the LBSCR became chairman of the Crystal Palace Company. The London, Chatham & Dover Railway got in on the act, much to the LBSCR's fury, by constructing its own line right up to the front of the Palace. There was an ornate subterranean connection, which still exists, between the site of the Palace and the former High Level station. The 4-mile High Level branch, opened on 1 August 1865, was a nominally independent company entitled The Crystal Palace & South London Junction Railway. The railway, of course, was speculative and ran through a fairly sparsely populated area catching only a few passengers. After the Palace was destroyed by fire in 1936, the potential traffic was even less. The branch was closed temporarily in both wars, from 1 January 1917 to 1 March 1919, and from 22 May 1944 to 4 March 1946.

The branch had been electrified on 12 July 1925, a substation being built at Upper Sydenham to feed both the High Level branch and the main line in Penge Tunnel underneath. Electrification did little to encourage patronage and the line was closed to all traffic by BR on 20 September 1954. A special last steam-hauled train was run on Sunday 19 September 1954, hauled by a SECR C class 0-6-0. Enormous crowds turned out to witness the event which was an extremely rare one – the closure of a passenger line in the London area. Today, parts of the line have been built over but there are relics to be seen, the best being the original station

buildings at Upper Sydenham opened in 1884 and now in use as a private residence.

Elmers End to Hayes and Addiscombe

The 3½-mile, South Eastern Railway country branch line from Elmers End to Hayes still flourishes and, although surrounded by suburbia, the massive overbridges and embankments still suggest the country branch line of 1882. Hayes station was rebuilt by the Southern just before World War II, in 1935, destroyed by bombing in 1940 (they were aiming for RAF Biggin Hill), and rebuilt again by the Southern Region in 1956. Eden Park must be unique for a Southern station in that there is no road to the station – access is by a footpath only. Eden Park is a beautiful survival of a South Eastern Railway country station constructed in Kentish weatherboard. The line, only 3½ miles long, was opened on 29 May 1882 through rural Kentish countryside, but after electrification in 1925 housing development took off, and as a result the line prospered.

Addiscombe was opened in 1864, the same year as Elmers End, and was known as Croydon (Addiscombe Road) until 1 April 1925 when renamed by the Southern Railway. The line was electrified in 1926 and a large carriage depot for multiple unit stock erected. The 2-mile line today still has a service but will become part of the new Tramlink system. New Beckenham old station, closed in 1864, still survives as a private house known appropriately as Station House. The line has recently been singled.

Upper Sydenham, on the former Crystal Palace High Level branch, shows the scene in 1954 and shortly afterwards when the platform buildings were demolished. The station house of 1884 is still in use as a private residence. The line closed on 20 September 1954.

Top photograph by J. H. Aston

Crystal Palace High Level, as seen from above the tunnel shortly after closure which took place in September 1954. The sidings were used for storage of empty stock both electric and loco hauled. The site is now occupied by a housing estate but the retaining wall is still visible.

Lens of Sutton

Eden Park on the Hayes branch is a fine example of a South Eastern Railway Kentish weatherboard country station of the late 19th century. The station is unique to the Southern in that there is no road access.

Addiscombe signal box was one of the last South Eastern Railway weatherboard structures but has now been destroyed by fire. The line was, until recently, semaphore signalled but has now had the signalling removed and is operated as a single branch from Elmers End. It will soon be replaced by the Tramlink system.

Woodside to Selsdon

This 'Croydon avoiding line' was opened on 10 August 1885 from Woodside to Selsdon Road (2¼ miles) and was owned jointly by the LBSCR and the SER. Opened as the Woodside & South Croydon Railway, the line was worked on alternate years by the two owning companies. The line was closed in 1917 as a wartime economy. The Southern reopened and electrified the line as far as Sanderstead on 30 September 1935. Coombe Road and Bingham Road stations were rebuilt at this time but the SR had in mind the Southern Heights Light Railway when electrifying to Selsdon.

The Southern Heights Light Railway was a scheme for an electrified light railway to run from Sanderstead to Orpington with eight intermediate stations. The famous light railway promoter Colonel Stephens had a hand in the scheme but his death in 1931 caused the proposal to fail as the capital had not been raised. The Southern Railway was to work the line which was even shown on Southern carriage maps as a projected railway. The Woodside to Selsdon line closed to all traffic on 16 May 1983 and within a few months was totally demolished – no stations, no track, and partially dismantled bridges. This was one of the quickest branch line demolitions ever carried out. Part of the trackbed will be used by the new Tramlink system to connect Beckenham, New Addington and Wimbledon with Croydon.

Bromley North

The South Eastern Railway got to Bromley after the LCDR in 1878 with a short, 1½-mile, branch from Grove Park which was opened on 1 January 1878. The principal landowner on the line, a Mr Scott, insisted on a station being sited near his residence, Sundridge Park, for his convenience. The result was the two closest-together stations on BR, for Sundridge Park is only a ¼ mile from Bromley North – almost a train length. The line was electrified on 18 February 1926, the terminus having been rebuilt by the Southern in 1925. Today, the Southern Railway station at Bromley North, recently renovated, stands prominently in the town, a handsome brick building with copper covered cupola.

Epsom Downs

The line from Sutton to Epsom Downs (4¼ miles) was opened on 22 May 1865 – just in time for the Epsom races, and was double track throughout. Epsom Downs station had nine platforms in its heyday and the monopoly on race traffic until the Tattenham Corner line arrived in 1901. From 1901 the Epsom Downs line also lost its royal trains to the rival branch. The branch was worked by LBSCR railmotors until electrification on 17 June 1928, although overhead ac wiring had been put up on part of the line, but was never used. Disaster struck the branch on 16 November 1981 when Epsom Downs signal box was destroyed by fire – and the line has

13

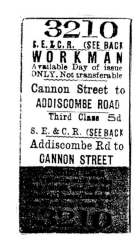

3210
S. E. & C. R. (SEE BACK
WORKMAN
Available Day of issue
ONLY. Not transferable
Cannon Street to
ADDISCOMBE ROAD
Third Class 5d
S. E. & C. R. (SEE BACK
Addiscombe Rd to
CANNON STREET

Hayes station was bombed during World War II and rebuilt afterwards by BR. The upper picture shows Hayes in recent times with a 4 EPB unit and the lower, in SECR days. The only feature to have survived are the buffer-stops.

Coombe Road on the former Woodside to Selsdon line shows the Southern station in 1983, and shortly after closure. The line will be used by the new Croydon Tramlink now under construction.

WOODSIDE, COOMBE LANE AND SELSDON ROAD.
(WORKED BY S. E. & C. COMPANY ON AND FROM JULY 1ST, 1904.)

UP. — WEEK DAYS ONLY.

M.C.		Eng a.m.	Eng a.m.	a.m.	a.m.	a.m.	a.m.	a.m.	Goods. p.m.	Goods. p.m.	p.m.	p.m.	p.m.	p.m.	Sats. only.	Not Sats.	Gds.	p.m.	Not Sats. p.m.	Sats. only. p.m.	B Goods p.m.	p.m.		Not Sats. p.m.	Sats. only. p.m.	p.m.
—	Selsdon Road dep.	552	641	733	811	9 5	1058	1221	123	140	238	255	3 0	6	350	4 16	5 35	5 50	5 55	5 51	7 30	7 41			8 20	
0 53	Coombe Lane „	G	...	735	813	9 7	11 0	1223	1 43		2 58	3 2	3 8	...		4 18	5 37	5 52	...	6 53	7 32	7 43			8 22	
2 33	Woodside arr.	559	647	739	817	911	11 4	1297	148	2 0	3 3	...	3 6	2 12	358	4 22	5 41	5 56	6 3	6 57	7 36	7 47			8 26	

DOWN. — WEEK DAYS ONLY.

		Goods. a.m.	a.m.	a.m.	a.m.	a.m.	a.m.	B Gds. p.m.	Sats. only. p.m.	Not Sats. p.m.	Sats. only. p.m.	Not Sats. p.m.	Sats. only. p.m.	Not Sats. p.m.	Sats. only. p.m.	Not Sats. p.m.	Sats. only. p.m.	Not Sats. p.m.	Sats. only. p.m.		Eng. p.m.	Eng. midt.
	Woodside dep.	550	6 0	720	755	845	1016	1113	1 10	121	1 25	3 40	3 50	4 57	5 4	6 15	6 31	7 12	7 21	7 40	7 53	845 1131 1241
	Coombe Lane „	...	...	723	759	49	1020	1117	...	125	1 29	3 44	3 54	5 1	5 8	6 19	6 35	7 16	7 25	7 44	7 57	... N T T
	Selsdon Rd. arr.	610	625	726	8 1	851	1022	1119	1 30	127	1 31	3 46	3 56	5 3	5 10	6 21	6 37	7 18	7 27	7 46	7 59	849 1138 1248

B Oxted Line Goods when required runs in place of 7.35 a.m. Down and 1.40 p.m. Up Goods.
G From Purley to Hayes. **N.T.** Thursdays excepted, Engine, Engine to Purley. **T** Saturdays excepted, Engine.
ENGINE HEAD BOARDS AND LIGHTS.
By Day — No Head Boards will be carried by Day.
By Night — The Engine will carry a White Light on near side end of Buffer Beam.

SELSDON ROAD TO SANDERSTEAD AND BACK.

Between its arrival at Selsdon Road at 10.27 a.m. and its departure at 11.0 a.m. the Woodside Branch Engine and Guard will work Trucks of Goods from that Station to Sanderstead, returning to Selsdon Road at once. This Engine also does the necessary Goods Yard shunting at Selsdon Road, and places Wagons in position for the 10.10 p.m Oxted to New Cross to take on.

An extract from the Winter 1904 LBSCR working timetable which shows both passenger and goods trains. The line was worked by the LBSCR and the SECR but was closed by BR in 1983. A section of the old trackbed will be used for part of the new tramway system centred on Croydon.

been single ever since. An interesting feature of Southern Railway days was the opening of intermediate signal boxes known as A, B and C; these were only open for the Epsom race week. The semaphore signals carried no spectacles as they were used in daylight hours only. These signals were abolished in 1955. The old station building has been demolished and the line cut back with a new terminus provided for the single track. Banstead goods yard is now a shooting club.

Caterham and Tattenham Corner

The Caterham branch (4¾ miles) was opened on 5 August 1856 for both goods and passengers. The Caterham Railway was an independent company initially, which the SER bought in 1859 after lengthy negotiations. The Southern Railway electrified the branch on 25 March 1928. The centenary of the opening was celebrated on 6 August 1956 with a steam special hauled by an AIX class 0-6-0T; the locomotive was built in 1878, formerly LBSCR No. 35 *Morden* and numbered DS 377. The engine was painted in Stroudley livery in 1947 and lettered *Loco Works Brighton* – regrettably the engine was broken up in September 1963. The Tattenham Corner line (8 miles) opened throughout in 1901, the section from Purley to Kingswood & Burgh Heath having been opened on 2 November 1897 and from there to Tadworth on 1 July 1900. The chairman of the SECR, Cosmo Bonsor, happened to live at Kingswood and no doubt had some influence over the construction of the line and the grandiose station at Kingswood, itself a delight of late Victorian architecture. Tattenham Corner opened on Derby Day, 4 June 1901, had six platforms, three signal boxes and a special grandstand right outside the station. From the prestige point of view, the SECR also stole the royal trains from the 'Brighton' and to this day

Bromley North station has been restored and is a fine example of a Southern Railway structure of the twenties. The station was rebuilt in 1925 for the electrification.

Epsom Downs originally had nine platforms, but the old building has now been demolished and a new single platform has been built on a new site short of the original station.

Tattenham Corner showing the original building of 1901 which was built to take large crowds for the race course which was right outside the station. The building, which was demolished a few years ago when a train overan the platform, has since been replaced.

Kingswood & Burgh Heath station was unique. The SECR opened the line from Purley in 1897 and the stations were individually designed. The railway wanted to encourage day trippers into the countryside and a tearoom and terrace were built over the platform canopy. The tea terrace was in use until World War I.

the Queen still travels in a special train to Tattenham Corner ever year for the Derby. The regular service to Tattenham Corner lasted until 1907 but was withdrawn until 1928 when the Southern Railway electrified this 8¼-mile long branch. An unusual feature on the line was the tea terrace on the station canopy at Kingswood, possibly unique on a British railway

station although common practice in India. The SECR encouraged day trippers to the Chipstead Valley and the tea terrace was provided at Kingswood until the First World War. The new station building at Tattenham Corner is in good repair (where it comes under royal scrutiny), but the others on the branch have become tatty.

Branch Lines to the South West of London

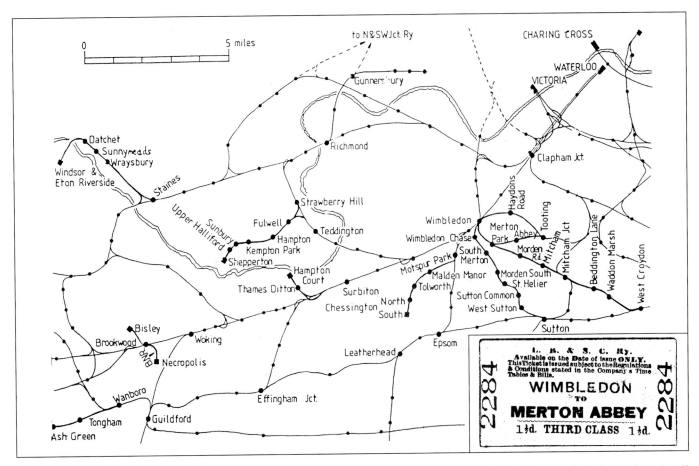

West Croydon to Wimbledon

A 6¼-mile cross-country line mostly single track which, before being engulfed by London suburbia, could have been termed 'a branch line'. Even today, the line has a rural appearance about it not associated with suburban lines. The line was opened on 22 October 1855 and electrified on 6 July 1930, the multiple unit trains displacing the push-and-pull service inaugurated by the LBSCR in 1919. Electrification has probably saved the line from closure, the 2 SUB units that were introduced were conversions from the South London line stock of 1909. These units had a long internal side corridor, a feature of LBSCR rolling stock. The West Croydon

Mitcham on the Wimbledon to West Croydon line with two-car ex LBSCR stock, set No. 1805, in BR days. The station building at street level has reverted to a private house and the line awaits redevelopment.
Lens of Sutton

South Merton has changed over the years as the picture (above) shows the line on opening in 1929 with a Southern three-car electric unit with 'H' headcode. The illustration below shows the scene today (November 1996). The line is now operated by Thameslink with Class 319 units and the station is somewhat overgrown. The milepost, left, remains in situ.

Top photograph by H. F. Wheeller

Merton Abbey station with a railtour in 1958, headed by H class 0-4-4T No. 31521, on what is now a road. The line closed to passengers in 1929 and freight in 1975. Little remains to be seen of the former line, but part of the trackbed at the Merton Park end is now a footpath.

Merton Park was the junction for the Merton Abbey line seen here on the left. It was closed to passengers in 1929. This scene, taken in 1985 showing set No. 6328, has changed as the former branch is now overgrown and the two-car stock has been replaced. The line will become part of the Wimbledon to Croydon Tramlink system.

Merton Abbey sees H class 0-4-4T No. 31521 of 1909 on a Southern Counties Touring Society special, the 'South Londoner', in 1958. The passenger service was withdrawn on 3 March 1929 and freight ceased on 5 May 1975. The site is now a road and roundabout.

to Wimbledon line is built partially over the course of the Surrey Iron Railway of 1804 – the world's first public railway. One or two features of this historic line can still be seen. The station building at Mitcham, formally a private house, has Tramway Path alongside it, as also does the Surrey Iron Hackbridge branch. The Hackbridge branch of the Surrey Iron can still be discerned alongside the main road from Mitcham Common to Hackbridge. This must have been the first branch line on a public railway; the Surrey Iron was horse-worked and regarded as a public right of way, very much like a modern road. The Wimbledon to West Croydon line will become part of the local Tramlink system in the future.

Merton Park to Tooting Junction
Prior to electrification of the Tooting to Wimbledon lines in 1929, the service to Wimbledon was on a loop line via Merton Abbey or Haydons Road. The line was known by railway staff as the Wimbledon 'pear'. With electrification, the Merton Abbey section was closed on 3 March 1929, the line having been closed from 1917 to 1923 anyway. The opening of the Northern Line of London Transport in 1926 did a lot to kill off the passenger traffic potential on the line. The 1½-mile Merton Abbey branch did stay open to freight until 5 May 1975 having been opened jointly by the LBSCR and the LSWR on 1 October 1868. Today, the line has been built over

and obliterated by a road from the station site to Morden Road.

The Wimbledon & Sutton Railway
This 5¼-mile suburban link from the former LSWR main line at Wimbledon to Sutton was opened for traffic on 5 January 1930 and was electrified from the outset. The line could hardly be termed a branch line but had many features common to the forthcoming Chessington branch of 1939. The Wimbledon & Sutton was built to keep the District Railway out of Sutton and more importantly the Northern Line, Morden extension away from Southern territory. Today, the Northern Line terminates almost head on with the Wimbledon & Sutton near Morden South. The large housing estates of the twenties justified the construction of the line which has island platform stations. The steepest part of the line is the 1 in 44 between West Sutton and Sutton over which steam locomotives were banned.

Chessington South
This railway opened throughout on 28 May 1939 and was one of the Southern's showpieces. The stations were built in concrete and had awnings entitled 'Chisarc cantilevered reinforced concrete', similar to LT stations in the outer suburbs. This 4¼-mile long line is certainly thriving and, peering over the fences of some of the intermediate stations,

Tolworth station was on the Southern's showpiece line which opened on 29 May 1938 and was extended to Chessington South on 28 May 1939. The stations were constructed in concrete and were designed to take large crowds.

Lens of Sutton

Chessington South was opened on 28 May 1939, and the line was originally going to be built through to Leatherhead but the 1939-1945 war prevented further construction.

Hampton Court was one of the earliest LSWR branch lines, and was opened in 1849. The building, built to the design of William Tite, has been modified and the canopies cut back.

Kempton Park on the Shepperton branch sees modern stock in this December 1985 view, but the station is not open to the general public as it serves the racecourse only, which is adjacent. The line was opened in November 1864 and was electrified in 1916. The station was opened in 1878 by the LSWR.

Windsor & Eton Riverside is still intact and in 1957 witnessed a rare event when ex LBSCR 'Remembrance' class No. 32331 *Beattie* arrived on a boy scouts excursion. There were only seven engines in the class which were 4-6-0s rebuilt from the old LBSCR 4-6-4Ts.

The 'Bisley Bullet' at Brookwood in Southern Railway days with Stroudley D1 class 0-4-2T No. 2260 and LSWR push-and-pull set. The branch did not have a regular service but was shown on the SR maps.

Above and opposite: Two views of Bisley taken on 23 November 1952, the occasion of the RCTS railtour. The station is still intact today and is owned by Lloyds Bank who use it as a pavilion for their rifle team. The track is now occupied by a former BR sleeping car which provides accommodation for visitors.

Hugh Ballantyne

the passenger has the impression of endless suburbia spreading for miles and miles over the horizon. The line was intended to go through to Leatherhead but the 1939-1945 war knocked that on the head and the line today terminates at Chessington South which was designed to be an intermediate station. The branch terminates so abruptly that within a few minutes' walk the passenger finds himself in open country with suburbia behind him.

Hampton Court

The short branch, of only 2 miles, from Hampton Court Junction on the main line, crosses the four-track main line on the handsome brick-built viaduct of 1915. The Hampton Court line was included in the first round of LSWR electrification (1915-1916). The line was electrified on 18 June 1916 on 660 volt dc current with conductor rail. Hampton Court station, in Victorian gothic, was opened on 1 February 1849 and looks rather tatty today.

Shepperton

This 7¼-mile line was mooted as the Thames Valley Railway and opened on 1 November 1864, the LSWR taking over in

1865. The line was one of the first to be electrified by the LSWR, being opened for electric traction on 30 January 1916. The LSWR had adopted the third rail dc scheme following a visit by officials to study the New York system. The Americans must have done a good selling job to the railway as it later resulted in the system being adopted as standard for the whole of the Southern. (Perhaps it is a pity that the LSWR did not adopt an overhead electrification system, as every railwayman and traveller can testify to this day.) An unusual feature of the Shepperton branch is the station at Kempton Park which has no public access, not even a footpath! The station is used for the races and was opened in 1878 although the present structure probably dates from the 1890 rebuild.

Windsor & Eton Riverside

Windsor & Eton was opened on 1 December 1849, and was 6¾ miles from Staines. The station had a fine gothic terminal building of an individual design, the architect being Sir William Tite. The line was electrified on 6 July 1930. The section of Waterloo station where Windsor and Reading trains terminated was known as the Windsor lines, together with the four tracks from Waterloo to Clapham Junction. The Reading line opened

in 1856 and this subsequently became the main line hence the sharp curve when leaving Staines in the down direction.

Bisley

This 1½-mile branch was opened from Brookwood on 12 July 1890 to Bisley Camp for the National Rifle Association which had been transferred from Wimbledon Common. The branch was not advertised in the public timetable but was shown on Southern Railway maps and was closed to all traffic on 21 July 1952. The line was rail-toured with a push-and-pull unit after closure. The station survives today and is owned by Lloyds Bank Rifle Club who provide a BR sleeping coach on a short length of track for overnight visitors. Bisley Camp provides a taste of the old Raj as it is reminiscent of an Indian hill station.

Brookwood Necropolis

The Brookwood Cemetery branch was opened in 1854 and trains were run from a special station alongside the LSWR terminus at Waterloo. This had two platforms with the entrance in Westminster Bridge Road. From here the LSWR ran through trains for the Necropolis Company to the cemetery which had two stations. Trains ran until 1941 but in May of that year the train and station at Waterloo were destroyed by bombing. The stations at the cemetery were intact until recently, but the south station was destroyed by fire in September 1972, the north having already been demolished.

A curious feature was that each corpse was issued with a ticket for the journey from Waterloo – no returns, only singles! Part of the line today is a public footpath.

Branch Lines in Kent

Gravesend West Street

This 4½-mile long branch was opened as late as 17 April 1886 by the LCDR, the rival South Eastern Railway having got to Gravesend in 1849 by the North Kent Railway. There were three intermediate stations on the line: Longfield, Southfleet and Rosherville which was built to serve the nearby Rosherville Gardens, a resort for day trippers. Rosherville closed on 15 July 1933 after having been reduced to a halt status. A feature of the line was that boat trains ran from 1916 to 1940 to connect with a boat to Holland. The train started from Victoria, included a Pullman and was usually short enough to be hauled by an H class 0-4-4 tank. The line closed to passenger traffic on 3 August 1953. Freight traffic over the line lasted until 29 March 1968, from Southfleet to Gravesend, the section from Southfleet closing on 26 January 1976 to Fawkham Junction.

Westerham

This was another rural South Eastern Railway branch which nearly made it to the preservation scene and, had the line been preserved, it would have been a great success as it was near to London and could take the largest locomotives - even Bulleid 4-6-2s. The line was opened amid much ceremony on 6 July 1881 and was one of the first to have steam railmotors which were introduced in April 1906. Push-and-pull working with SECR standard P or H classes followed and this was the method of line working right up to complete closure which was from 30 October 1961. The closure of the line was hastened by political interests as the present M25 motorway runs over most of the site of the line. A preservation society was formed, the Westerham Valley Railway Association, but little co-operation was offered by the authorities as the Sevenoaks bypass and M25 needed the railway land. There

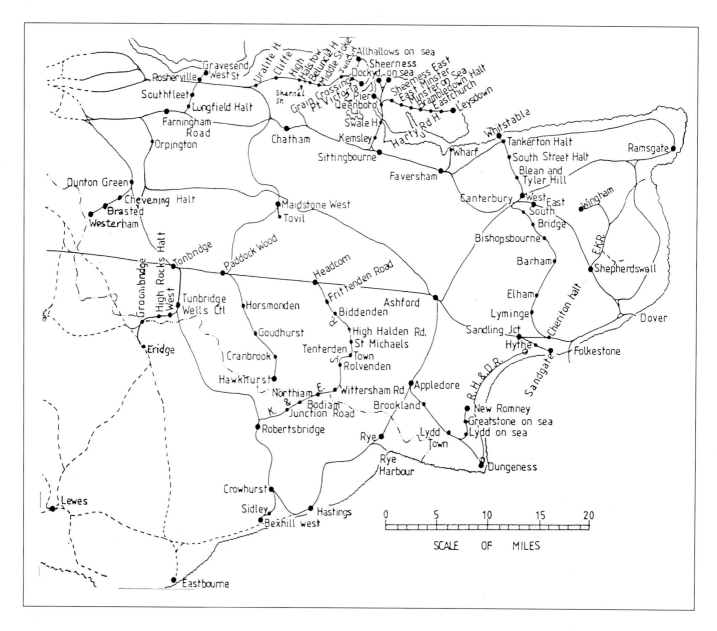

Gravesend West St. station with E1 class 4-4-0 No. 31507 on an RCTS special in March 1959. The special train originated from Liverpool Street, hence the Gresley stock seen here in a mixture of red and cream, and maroon livery. The station closed to normal passenger services on 3 August 1953 but stayed open for freight until 29 March 1968

Longfield Halt was one of the intermediate stations on the Gravesend West St. branch of the former London, Chatham & Dover Railway. The all-timber halt was opened by the SECR on 1 July 1913 and closed with the end of the passenger service on 3 August 1953.

Westerham on 11 April 1952 with R1 class 0-4-4T No. 31704 and ex SECR push-and-pull set No. 481 which started life as a steam railmotor. The R1 class were an LCDR design, but this example was built during the SECR era after the amalgamation. The engine survived until April 1956 as the last example of the class.

S. C. Nash

Dunton Green bay platform a year before closure, with H class 0-4-4-T No. 31512 waiting for the connection prior to setting off for Westerham. Built at Ashford in 1909 the engine was withdrawn in June 1961.

Hugh Ballantyne

Westerham in June 1960 with ex SECR H class No. 31512 and an LBSCR two-coach push-and-pull set. The line closed to all traffic on 30 October 1961 and would have been preserved had it not been for the M25 motorway which was to cover most of the former branch.

Hugh Ballantyne

Hawkhurst station in May 1961, shortly before closure, with H class 0-4-4T No. 31500 about to propel the train to Paddock Wood. The branch opened in 1893 and was built to keep the rival LCDR out of Hastings. The line actually terminated at Gills Green which was a long way from Hawkhurst town.

CLOSURE OF HAWKHURST BRANCH RAILWAY LINE

On and from MONDAY, 12th JUNE 1961, all services will be withdrawn from the Hawkhurst branch line and HORSMONDEN, GOUDHURST, CRANBROOK and HAWKHURST stations, also Churn Lane and Pattenden sidings, closed.

British Railways will continue to provide collection and delivery services for parcels and freight sundries throughout the area and facilities for truck load traffic exist at other stations in the vicinity.

Further information may be obtained from the Station Master at PADDOCK WOOD (Telephone: 322) or TONBRIDGE (Telephone: 2266) or from the Line Traffic Manager, Southern Region, British Railways, South Eastern Division, 61 Queen Street, London, E.C.4.
(Telephone: WATerloo 5151, Ext. 227).

Enquiries in regard to bus services in the area should be addressed to:-

The Maidstone & District Motor Services Ltd.
Knightrider House, Maidstone   · Telephone: 2211
St. John's Road, Tunbridge Wells   20221
Opera House Buildings, Tunbridge Wells   1700
Sandhurst Road, Hawkhurst   3169

A general view of the Hawkhurst terminus in May 1961 with a Maunsell set in the single platform. The signal box survives in what is now a timber yard.

was, however, some small benefit in that an H class 0-4-4 and C class 0-6-0 were bought for the line and can now be seen running on the Bluebell Railway in Sussex. These two locomotives have been restored to their SECR Brunswick green and are numbered 263 and 592 respectively. The branch to Westerham (4¾ miles) was always popular with visiting enthusiasts.

Paddock Wood to Hawkhurst

The Hawkhurst branch could be described as everybody's favourite. The line was steam-worked, single-track, passed through picturesque countryside and ran from nowhere to nowhere. The line left the main line at Paddock Wood and headed off southwards across the Kentish hopfields. There were three intermediate stations, at Horsmonden, Goudhurst and Cranbrook, on the 11½-mile journey to Hawkhurst. The South Eastern Railway promoted the line and opened it on 4 September 1893 for they were determined to keep the LCDR out of their territory. The railway was engineered by the then youthful Holman F. Stephens who was appointed at the age of

Last days at Cranbrook with the staff being collected on 10 June 1961 by the crew of C class No. 31588 and SECR push-and-pull set No. 656. The rural station has survived as a private residence and is owned by a Calor gas distributor.
E. Wilmshurst

Goudhurst on the Hawkhurst branch with ex SECR H class No. 31324 propelling to Paddock Wood on Tonbridge duty No. 304. The station has now disappeared and little remains to be seen of the former railway. Note that the oil lamps on the platform are being prepared for the evening.

C class No. 31592 approaches Horsmonden on 2 May 1961 with the Hawkhurst goods, shortly before closure. The engine was built at Longhedge in 1902 and is the sole survivor of the class having been in use on the Bluebell Railway since 1970.

S. C. Nash

Horsmonden station on the Hawkhurst branch with H class No. 31500 of 1905 on 6 May 1961 not long before the branch closed to all traffic. The engine was withdrawn a month later and the station buildings are now a garage and vehicle test centre.

The Hawkhurst branch traversed the Kentish hop fields and two old veterans, D1 class 4-4-0 No. 31735 and C class 0-6-0 No. 31244, can be seen double-heading with a collection of SECR coaches on 20 September 1953. This empty stock formed a hop pickers' return excursion from Hawkhurst to London Bridge.

S. C. Nash

More empty stock, en route to Goudhurst is seen near Churn Lane on 20 September 1951, hauled by D1 class No. 31741 and D class No. 31734. The train worked double-headed back to London Bridge with the D class leading the ex SECR 'birdcage' set. No. 31734 was withdrawn from service in October 1955 and was intended for preservation but was found to be defective, so No. 31737 was saved instead.

S. C. Nash

C class No. 31588 works the last train over the Hawkhurst branch on 20 June 1961. The engine was picking up goods vehicles that had been left on the line since closure a week earlier on 12 June.

G. Daniels

35

22 as resident engineer. Later, as Colonel Stephens, he was to manage and build a large number of light railways throughout the country.

Hawkhurst was originally planned for electrification on the Stage 2 Kent Electrification schemes of the 1960s, but owing to financial cutbacks something had to go. It would be interesting to see what the line would be like today had it been electrified. A curious feature of the line in steam days were the hop-pickers specials from London Bridge, usually worked by an ancient SECR locomotive and true to form, running via very devious routes to get to the branch. Mechanisation of hop picking did away with this unusual traffic shortly before the line closed to all traffic on 12 June 1961. Today, Horsmonden station can still be seen and is in use as a local garage. Cranbrook is now a private house in a Calor gas distribution depot. Hawkhurst station has been demolished but the signal box still survives, having been restored and repainted. Goudhurst station site has been erased.

Allhallows and Grain

The South Eastern Railway opened up Port Victoria station and pier on 11 September 1882, 11½ miles from Hoo Junction on the Isle of Grain. The rival LCDR had opened a station on the opposite side of the Medway at Queenborough Pier on 15 May 1876. Port Victoria was used by boat trains until May 1904, thereafter only local branch trains to Gravesend were operated on the line which was also used by royalty. It was popular with Queen Victoria as few people could get there to see the royal trains. The ordinary passenger services to Port Victoria were discontinued on 11 June 1951, the pier having slipped quietly into the Medway. From 4 September 1951 a new station was opened at Grain for the workers at the nearby oil refinery which had a vast acreage. Passenger services to Grain and Allhallows ceased on 4 December 1961. The oil network at Grain now obliterates all signs of the former SER Port Victoria line but trains still run to Grain from Hoo Junction although the BP refinery ceased operating in 1983. A strange twist in the fortunes of the branch is that now North Sea oil is used, there is no need to import Middle East oil at this location.

The Grain branch was connected by a new line from Stoke Junction to Allhallows, opened by the Southern Railway on 16 May 1932. This 1¾-mile long line was promoted by the Southern with the intention of capturing the commuter, holiday and day tripper traffic to the new speculative beach resort of Allhallows-on-Sea. The intended property development did not take place and the line was closed to all traffic on 4 December 1961 by BR who have since demolished the stations. Now, 35 years later, the inevitable has happened. Property development has increased, holiday

A bank holiday excursion worked by C class No. 31086 forms the 12.41pm Erith to Allhallows near Cliffe in 1954. A mixture of old SECR stock headed by a birdcage brake trails behind the ageing 0-6-0 which was built at Ashford in 1900 and withdrawn from service by BR in October 1960.

S. C. Nash

Cliffe on 2 December 1961 shortly before closure. H class No. 31530 departs with a Gravesend train consisting of converted Maunsell stock. Cliffe was one of the original stations of 1882. The H class lasted until March 1962.

High Halstow Halt on 2 December 1961 just before closure of the Allhallows line. The halts on the line were rebuilt by the Southern Railway in concrete during the 1930s. This halt was situated at Wybourne Crossing and the signal box retained that name until the line closed.

Sharnall Street was the terminus of the line until it was extended to Port Victoria. The station was also a crossing point on the single line. In this view, taken in the 1930s, a pristine H class 0-4-4T blows off whilst waiting to take the train on to Allhallows. No. 1308 was built in 1906 and lasted until December 1962 as BR No. 31308.

Lens of Sutton

Ivatt Class 2 2-6-2T No. 41300 leaves Sharnall Street on 24 August 1952 with an excursion from the London suburbs to Allhallows. The station has disappeared but the line still runs through the site. Note the milk churns on the platform.

D. Trevor Rowe

Beluncle Halt on the Allhallows line was opened by the SECR in 1906 to cater for the steam railmotor service. The timber structure was replaced by the Southern in the thirties. The halt was named after a nearby farm. This view is dated 5 June 1928.

H. A. Vallance

Middle Stoke Halt in Southern concrete, as seen just prior to closure on 2 December 1961. The halt was originally opened by the SECR in 1906 but it was rebuilt by the Southern.

Stoke Junction Halt with H class No. 31324 and a Maunsell push-and-pull set on 2 December 1961. No. 31324, built in 1907, survived until July 1962 and is seen propelling out of the single platform for Allhallows. Note the bags of coal in the yard.

Allhallows-on-Sea was the Southern Railway's great hope for the future as the company wanted to develop a new seaside resort to rival Southend on the other side of the water. H class No. 31158 is seen in the platform with ex LBSCR coaches forming a two-coach push-and-pull set. The engine was withdrawn in 1955, the station closed on 4 December 1961 and the site built over. A mobile homes park covers the spot where the station once stood.

S. C. Nash

Grain, with H class No. 31517 in January 1960 about to depart with the 11.37am to Gravesend Central. The station opened on 10 June 1951 to serve the new oil refinery and replaced the old Port Victoria terminus. Grain is still the terminus of the line but the station was closed to passengers on 4 December 1961.

H class No. 31324 leaves Grain with the 11.37am to Gravesend Central on 2 December 1961, shortly before closure. The oil refinery can be seen in the background

S. C. Nash

caravan parks have been built and new estates, shops and schools constructed - the whole place is booming! The perfect irony is that Kingsmead Park caravan park is located where the station once stood - only the water tower survives to remind residents that this was once the site of the railway. The Southern Railway was right but they opened the Allhallows line about 60 years too soon!

The Sheppey Light Railway (Leysdown-Queenborough)

This standard gauge branch of 8¾ miles, ran eastwards from Queenborough on the Sheerness line and was constructed as a light railway under the 1896 Act, the engineer being H. F. Stephens. The line opened for traffic on 1 August 1901 and became part of the SECR network. The intermediate stations had the Colonel Stephens look about them - with the use of corrugated iron and timber materials, the structures were cheaper than brick or stone. The SECR bought a LBSCR AIX class 0-6-0T, No. 654, for use on the line in 1905 and this was numbered into SECR stock as No. 751. This locomotive is now in Montreal at the Canadian Railroad Museum. The SECR tried steam railmotors but they had limited fuel and water capacity, so conventional SER or LCDR locomotives were used until closure on 4 December 1950 to all traffic. At closure the articulated push-and-pull railmotor sets were still in use - these were conversions from the SECR steam railcars of 1905 and lasted well into BR days. The articulated sets could also be seen at work on the Westerham branch well into the 1950s. Little evidence of the Leysdown branch can be seen today as the line had fairly light engineering works and a great deal of the old trackbed has been lost to view by being ploughed up by farmers.

Sheerness and Queenborough Pier

The 8-mile Sheerness branch opened on 19 July 1860. The connection with the main line at Sittingbourne faced London and gave direct running to Sheerness from the London direction, coming into use in 1863. Access to Sheerness on the Isle of Sheppey was over the Swale at Kingsferry Bridge which had a lifting section to allow ships to pass. This bridge was so decrepit that it was always jamming and causing considerable disruption to South Eastern Division services during the years prior to electrification in 1959. The Kingsferry Bridge was rebuilt and now carries road and rail together. The LCDR built a short branch to Queenborough Pier which was opened on 15 May 1876. A boat train service was provided which connected with the Zeeland Steamship Company's service to Flushing in Holland. The pier closed to all traffic on 1 March 1923 while Sheerness Dockyard had closed just before Grouping, on 2 January 1922.

A spotless R1 class 0-4-4T, No. 1697, at Sheerness on 2 June 1936 heads an all SECR train in SR green livery. No. 1697 was built in November 1900 by Sharp, Stewart to the LCDR design and was in a batch of 15 engines ordered by the SECR and survived until February 1953.

H. F. Wheeller

The SECR purchased an LBSCR A1 class 0-6-0T in 1905. Originally No. 54 *Waddon* it was re-numbered No. 751 in their stock and used on the Sheppey Light Railway that had opened on 1 August 1901. The 'Terrier' remained in service until 1963, latterly at Lancing Works where it was numbered 680S in BR departmental stock. It is now restored to LBSCR Stroudley livery and preserved at the Canadian Railroad Museum in Montreal.

Leysdown in Southern Railway days with C class No. 1252 on 2 June 1936. This engine was built in 1902 and lasted until 1959. The ex SECR stock was originally two steam railmotor vehicles of 1905 and was transferred to the Portland branch after the line closed on 4 December 1950. The Leysdown sets were the only articulated coaches on the Southern Railway.

H. F. Wheeller

A rural scene on the Sheppey Light Railway on 2 June 1936 as C class 0-6-0 No. 1252 waits for the guard to open the gates at Brambledown level crossing.

H. F. Wheeller

The Leysdown terminus of the Sheppey Light Railway on 2 June 1936 with the engine running round two-coach articulated set No. 514.

H. F. Wheeller

Interior views of coach No. 3561, one of the former steam railmotor vehicles on the Sheppey Light Railway during pre-war years. The coach was a saloon brake third of set No. 514. In the upper view the conductor/guard is seen walking the train and in the lower view is shown issuing bell punch tickets. In the background can be seen the driver's cab which was used when the unit was being propelled by pull-and-push fitted engines.

H. F. Wheeller

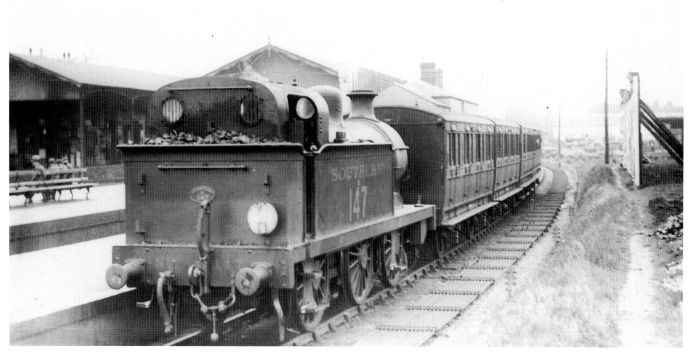

Canterbury West station sees R1 class 0-6-0T No. A147 in Southern Railway days. Some of the engines of the ex SER Stirling design of 1888 were modified in the 1930s with reduced boiler mountings and cut down cabs for working the Whitstable Harbour branch which had a low tunnel. The passenger train for Whitstable is seen in the bay platform with four-wheeled stock. The point rodding is quite amazing and must have been a difficult 'pull' for the signalman.

The Canterbury & Whitstable Railway

The first railway in Kent and one of the first public railways between two towns to be built for steam traction. The 6-mile line from Canterbury to Whitstable even preceded the Liverpool & Manchester Railway and was opened in May 1830, the Liverpool & Manchester opening six months later, in September. The line engineered by the Stephensons was mostly cable-worked with one level section worked by a steam locomotive *Invicta*, an 0-4-0, which was the 24th engine to be built by Robert Stephenson. The locomotive is now preserved in the Poor Priests Museum at Canterbury. The Canterbury & Whitstable line was bought by the South

The terminus of the Canterbury & Whitstable Railway was at Whitstable Harbour and R1 class No. 31339 is seen shunting at the old passenger station on 13 May 1950. The railway was opened on 4 May 1830 and predated the better known Liverpool & Manchester by six months.

S. C. Nash

The Canterbury & Whitstable Railway opened in 1830 and the bridge seen here near Whitstable & Tankerton station was reputed to be the first railway bridge over a road. A plaque to that effect was placed on the brickwork and can be seen in this 1959 view. The bridge has since been demolished due to road widening.

South Street Halt on the Canterbury & Whitstable branch was opened on 1 June 1911 by the SECR but closed on 1 January 1931, the day that the branch closed to passengers. Freights ran until 1 December 1952 although the line was reopened briefly in February 1953 owing to flooding on the LCDR route. The trackbed is now a footpath through a housing estate.

Lens of Sutton

Eastern Railway in 1853, passenger services ceased on 31 December 1930 and freight on 1 December 1952. The line had restricted clearances through Tyler Hill Tunnel which meant that the locomotives using the branch had to have cut down boiler mountings and cabs. A little known feature of the line was that the bridge over the public road at Whitstable, (by Whitstable & Tankerton station), had a plaque attached to the abutment claiming it to be the first rail over road bridge. It has now been demolished and the road widened.

Ramsgate Harbour and Margate Sands

The two old rivals, the LCDR and the SER, had duplicated the railway network in the Margate and Ramsgate area. The LCDR had a `main line' to Ramsgate Harbour (the building still exists) which was on the beach and reached over a steep gradient through a tunnel. The SER main line ran to Ramsgate Town but had a branch to Margate with some trains for Margate having to reverse in that station. With effect from 2 July 1926, the layout was simplified and trains could now run round the coast on a loop between Margate, Broadstairs and Ramsgate. The present Ramsgate station is on the site of the avoiding line.

Folkstone Harbour

This is a ¾-mile line from Folkestone Junction down to Folkestone Harbour on an average gradient of 1 in 30 - one of the steepest lines on the present system. The South Eastern Railway opened the line in 1849 having bought the harbour in 1843. The railway to Folkestone Harbour was one of the causes of Dover people backing the direct line from Dover to London, which later became the London, Chatham & Dover Railway, the South Eastern's cursed rival. Folkestone Harbour to Folkestone Junction was one of the most spectacular lines on BR for steam trains as they were worked by as many as four locomotives, sometimes two at the front and two at the back, but quite frequently by triple headers with one engine on the rear. Triple heading was extremely rare on a British railway - a sight not easily forgotten. The trains were worked by SER 0-6-0 R1 class tanks which, in 1959, were superseded by GWR pannier tanks. The line was electrified in 1961 but sees little traffic today.

The East Kent Light Railway (Shepherdswell-Wingham)

This was one of the Colonel Stephens lines in Kent, the first step in construction was to Tilmanstone Colliery just over a mile from Shepherdswell on the main LCDR Faversham to Dover line. Coal in Kent had been discovered when boring for a Channel Tunnel project, and Shepherdswell to Tilmanstone Colliery was opened on 27 November 1912. The passenger service to Wingham on the EKR was inaugurated on 16

Folkstone Harbour in the heyday of steam working where triple headers were a common sight. A trio of R1 class 0-6-0Ts headed by No. 31069 near the sidings at Folkestone Junction in this May 1956 view. The second engine has completely reduced boiler mountings for the Whitstable Harbour branch and the leading vehicle is an ex SECR boat saloon.

E. Wilmshurst

Folkestone Harbour sees ex South Eastern Railway R1 class 0-6-0T No. 31337 on 19 May 1957, the occasion of a visit by the SLS with a special train. The leading coach on the train is a SECR boat saloon behind which is a BR MkI and a Maunsell saloon. The line opened as early as 1849 and is still open but does not see the traffic density of former years.

The traditional scene on the Folkestone Harbour branch with two R1 class 0-6-0Ts struggling up the 1 in 30 gradient with the 'Golden Arrow' Pullman empties on 21 May 1956. The second engine has the cut down boiler mountings for the Canterbury & Whitstable branch.

G. Daniels

'Golden Arrow' empties arriving at Folkestone Harbour with R1 class 0-6-0T No. 31337. The line was famous for its 1 in 30 incline and triple headed trains. Steam finished with electrification in 1961.

E. Wilmshurst

An interesting townscape on the Folkestone Harbour branch with a GWR pannier tank shoving a boat train up the 1 in 30 bank at East Cliffe Crossing. Two other panniers are at the head of the train, seen here in 1961 just prior to electrification. The streets are unbelievably clear of traffic.

G. Daniels

Steam relics on the East Kent Railway in pre Nationalisation days with locomotives Nos 7, 8 and 2 at Shepherdswell. No. 7 was an 0-6-0ST built by Beyer Peacock in 1882 and of LSWR origin. The EKR bought the engine in 1924 and used it until 1941 when it was sent for scrap at Ashford. No. 8 was an ex SER O class 0-6-0 of 1891 purchased in 1928 and sold for scrap in 1934. No. 2 was an 0-6-0ST of 1908 built by Hudswell, Clarke and which lasted until 1959 having been sold to Purfleet Deep Wharf & Storage Co.

Lens of Sutton

Shepherdswell station on the East Kent Railway as seen in the heyday of the railway. The line was one of the Colonel Stephens systems and opened for passengers in 1916. The passenger service was withdrawn on 1 November 1948 but coal traffic lasted until 1986. In 1996 a limited passenger service was started by the East Kent Light Railway Society.

October 1916. An extension from Eastry on the Wingham line opened to Richborough Port on the coast near Pegwell Bay in December 1916. The Richborough line was to a wartime harbour including train ferries and extensive marshalling yards. The loading of the ships with wartime armaments and stores continued until the end of 1918, but an ordinary passenger service was not started until 1925 and only then to Sandwich Road. The East Kent built a station at Richborough but it was never used - in fact it never had any track. The Wingham line was extended to Canterbury Road in 1925 - a remote spot in the middle of nowhere, in fact 6 miles from Canterbury!

The Eastry to Sandwich Road branch closed on 1 November 1928 to passengers. Extensions to the system were planned on the premise that more collieries would be opened and a start was made on branches to Deal, Birchington and Canterbury but, with the death of Colonel Stephens in 1931, this work ceased. The Richborough Port section saw service again during World War II but was closed completely on 27 October 1949. The line from Canterbury Road closed to passengers on 1 November 1948; BR, the new owners, had not wasted much time in cutting out this uneconomic branch. By 1 July 1951 there was no freight beyond Tilmanstone, which was still open to the colliery until 1984, a distance of $2^{3}/_{4}$ miles.

The East Kent had a hotch-potch of secondhand locomotives and rolling stock which had mainly been purchased from the neighbouring Southern. An interesting survivor from this railway is former LSWR 4-4-2 No. 488, built in 1882 by Neilson & Co., which was acquired by the Bluebell Railway in 1961. In 1996 a small part of the East Kent Railway was reopened by the East Kent Light Railway Society. Trains were run from the August holiday weekend with a visiting locomotive from Mangapps Farm in Essex.

The Kent & East Sussex Railway (Headcorn to Robertsbridge)

This was probably the most successful of the Colonel Stephens group of railways and, like the East Kent, was nationalised on 1 January 1948. The KESR is also partly in use today, a regular service being run for most of the year from Tenterden using vintage locomotives and rolling stock. There is a museum at Tenterden featuring Colonel Stephens and his activities, including many personal relics. The line was opened in 1900 as the Rother Valley Railway from Robertsbridge to Rolvenden (then called Tenterden) and extended to Headcorn in 1904 as the KESR. The 24-mile railway lasted into BR days and was not closed to passengers until 4 January 1954. The section from Headcorn to Tenterden was closed to all traffic on that date and the remainder from Tenterden to Robertsbridge on 12 June 1961 to freight.

Early BR days, on the former Kent & East Sussex Railway, with Southern O1 class 0-6-0 No. 1064 on a classic mixed train at Rolvenden in 1949. The grubby O1 is in faded SR livery heading a SECR third brake with unfitted goods vehicles.

R. S. Carpenter

Rolvenden station in early Southern Region days with war time painting showing on the posts of the station building. In the background an ex SECR birdcage coach languishes in the bay platform. The scene today has changed but the pre-war atmosphere has been maintained.

R. S. Carpenter

AIX class 0-6-0T No. 377S of Brighton Works heads an LCGB special out of Rolvenden on 19 October 1958. AIX No. 32678 assists the train in the rear which comprises a mixed bag of pre-Grouping stock. No 377S was built at Brighton as No. 35 *Morden* in 1878, rebuilt to an AIX in 1922 and transferred to Brighton Works in 1946. The engine returned to ordinary stock in 1959 and was withdrawn by BR in 1963 as 32635. No. 32678 was built as No. 78 *Knowle* in 1880 and is now back on the KESR.

Rolvenden in pre-war years looked like a museum with bits and pieces of locomotives and rolling stock rusting away in the weeds. No. 1 *Tenterden*, a Hawthorn, Leslie 2-4-0T of 1899, is seen awaiting repair outside the shed in the 1930s. The engine was sold for scrap in 1941. A truly Colonel Stephens' scene.

Lens of Sutton

Southern 0-8-0T No. 949 *Hecate* is seen on Nine Elms loco shed with 0-6-0T No. 756 *A. S. Harris* in the 1930s. As KESR No. 4 *Hecate* was built by Hawthorn, Leslie in 1904, for the Maidstone extension but this did not materialise. The engine proved to be too big for the KESR and was sent to the Southern in 1932 where it worked until withdrawn in 1950. No. 756 was another 'one off' job having been built for the PD&SWJR in 1907 by the same firm.

R. S. Carpenter

Tenterden Town in BR days with ageing O1 class 0-6-0 No. 31064 arriving on a mixed train from Headcorn. The section from Headcorn to Tenterden was closed by BR to all traffic on 4 January 1954.

Tenterden Town in 1957 when the section to Robertsbridge was open to freight traffic only. AIX No. 32678, an ex K&ESR engine, waits to return with an empty van and brake. The line was freight only from January 1954 until complete closure in June 1961.

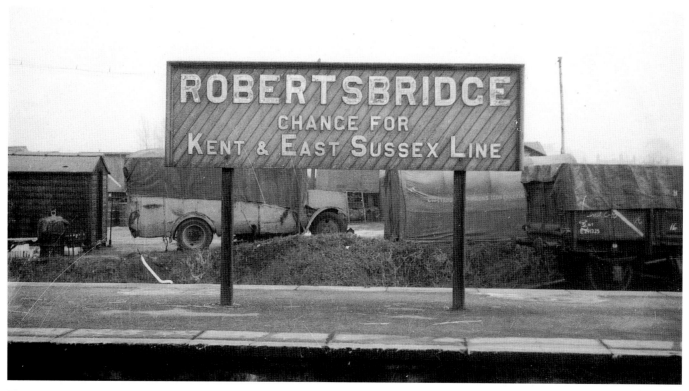

The ornate station nameboard at Robertsbridge on the down side with vintage vehicles in the goods yard. It advised passengers to change for the Kent & East Sussex Line, even in BR days.

A dated scene at Robertsbridge shows AIX No. 32678 waiting in the bay platform on 14 September 1957 with a hop pickers' special to Tenterden. The diesel electric multiple units on the Hastings line were introduced at about this time so the scene is certainly a rare one as the hop pickers' specials did not last for much longer.

G. Daniels

Dungeness was a desolate spot and the passenger service started by the South Eastern Railway in 1883 hung on until 4 July 1937, following the re-alignment of the New Romney line by the SR. Strangely enough, the line is still partly in use as an access route to the power station.

In 1961 the Kent & East Sussex Railway Association was formed and after lengthy negotiations, court cases, and a change of government, the line eventually received its Light Railway Transfer Order and reopened as the Tenterden Railway Company on 3 February 1974. This says much for the tenacity and determination of railway preservationists and the hope for the future is to extend the line to Bodiam where there is a fine moated castle a short walk from the station. The present line runs from Tenterden to Northiam, a spot in the middle of nowhere. The present KESR has a varied collection of locomotives and rolling stock including three AIX class 0-6-0Ts, one of which was an original KESR engine, being ex-LBSCR No. 70 *Poplar* of 1872 vintage. This engine was working until recently and was one of the oldest regularly worked locomotives. Colonel Stephens would be proud of the present set-up if he could see it today!

New Romney and Dungeness

The line from Appledore, on the Ashford to Hastings line, was opened for freight on 7 December 1881 to Dungeness (11 miles) and for passengers on 1 April 1883. The New Romney branch (4 miles) opened on 19 June 1884 for all traffic. Both Dungeness and New Romney became part of the South Eastern Railway system, the Lydd Railway Company having been absorbed in 1895. The SER proposed to open a port at Dungeness and run a steamer service to France.

The New Romney and Dungeness branches were certainly unusual as they ran from Lydd Town across miles and miles of shingle - a relic of the sea which has receded over the course of several centuries. New Romney and Rye were at one time on the coast. The Southern Railway realigned the New Romney line in June 1937 and brought the whole line nearer to the coastal stretch. They also opened new stations at Lydd and Greatstone-on-Sea hoping to tap the traffic from the coastal holiday camps which sprang up in the 1920s to 1930s.

The 15in gauge Romney, Hythe & Dymchurch Railway was opened along the coast from Dungeness to New Romney in 1929 and, of course, still runs today as a popular tourist attraction. New Romney survived into the diesel age and eventually closed to all traffic from New Romney to Lydd-on-Sea on 6 March 1967 but part of the Dungeness branch is still used by trains for the power station. An unusual event of

Lydd Town on the New Romney branch was a crossing point on the single-track line. In this scene an H class 0-4-4T crosses a Class 2 2-6-2T, No. 84020 on No. 364 duty of Ashford. The line closed to passengers on 6 March 1967.

J. H. Aston

Brookland was at one time a passing place on the Appledore to New Romney branch, but in this scene has been reduced to halt status. Opened on 7 December 1881 the line closed on 6 March 1967.

Lens of Sutton

Lydd-on-Sea Halt (for Dungeness) was opened for traffic on 4 July 1937 and was built with standard Southern Railway components. Dungeness was closed with the realignment of the New Romney branch and provision of new stations at Lydd and Greatstone.

Lens of Sutton

The exterior of New Romney station in BR days with regional signs adorning the South Eastern Railway building of 1884. The branch closed to all traffic on 6 March 1967, from here to Lydd Town.

Lens of Sutton

Bridge station on the Elham Valley line, in 1974, was in a good state of repair having been converted into a private house. The building, constructed in the economic materials of the time, survived the closure of 1940.

recent years was a Branch Line Society special with a 6L DEMU set which ran from Appledore to Dungeness on Saturday, 19 January 1985. The fare for the two trips to the power station siding was a mere £6.95 return for the 9½-mile journey. This was certainly a coup for the society as the Southern Region were reluctant to allow passenger trains over goods-only lines. New Romney station site is now an industrial estate but Lydd station still stands.

The Elham Valley Railway (Canterbury West-Shorncliffe)
The branch line from Canterbury to Folkestone, Harbledown Junction to Cheriton Junction to be precise, was 16¼ miles in length and traversed picturesque unspoilt Kentish countryside. The line was built mainly to keep the rival London, Chatham & Dover Railway away from the South Eastern's territory and was opened on 1 July 1889. The line had a chequered career. During World War II the Elham Valley was taken over by the Army and a rail-mounted 16-inch naval gun trundled up and down the line, occasionally firing off shells. The Luftwaffe were always trying to find the gun which was used to shell France, and several incidents occurred with the line being bombed or shot up. The Imperial War Museum has a

photograph of the Prime Minister inspecting the gun at Bishopsbourne in 1941. The Southern Railway closed the line to all traffic from 16 June 1947. Two of the stations survive today, having been converted into private houses. Bishopsbourne, the third station down the branch from Canterbury, was the station where Eustace Missenden, a future General Manager of the Southern Railway, started work as a ticket clerk in 1899. Elham station is now the local library.

Hythe and Sandgate
This 3-mile branch was opened on 9 October 1874, from Sandling Junction to Sandgate, with an intermediate station at Hythe. The South Eastern Railway ran a connecting horse tram from Sandgate to Hythe where the SER station was somewhat inconveniently situated for the town. Sandgate closed on 1 April 1931 and the line from Hythe to Sandling Junction went on 3 December 1951. The branch platform can still be seen at Sandling.

Miscellaneous lines
The London, Chatham & Dover Railway opened a short branch to Faversham Creek in April 1860 for goods traffic.

Bishopsbourne on the former South Eastern Railway's Elham Valley branch of 1889, presents a tranquil sight in this picture taken in Southern Railway days. The track has been singled but the station nameboard on the disused platform is still in situ. The building later became a house.

Lyminge, on the former Elham Valley line, in Southern days before closure, shows a few artifacts from the former SECR from the station signs to the canopy valancing. The South Eastern Railway opened the line throughout in 1889 but it was closed by the Southern Railway to all traffic on 16 June 1947. The line was built by the SER as a blocking line to keep the rival LCDR out of Folkestone.

Lens of Sutton

The Hythe branch is seen shortly before closure with ex LCDR R class 0-4-4T No. 31671, built in 1891 and withdrawn in 1954. The branch was opened by the South Eastern Railway in 1874 and closed by BR on 3 December 1951. The line originally went through to Sandgate but was cut back to Hythe on 1 April 1931.

A. Burgess

The Hythe branch train has arrived at Sandling Junction in this August 1949 photograph, headed by D3 class No. 32380. The ex LBSCR 0-4-4T is still in Southern Railway livery but with BR numbering. The set behind the engine is also of LBSCR origin. The bay platform still exists but the trackbed is overgrown.

S. C. Nash

Chatham Dockyard had an obscure branch line which left the main line in Gillingham and had no regular passenger service, although specials were run from time to time. Three C class 0-6-0s are seen hard at work on a cadets' special for London Bridge on 18 May 1959. Nos 31721 and 31495 lead the train of Maunsell stock, assisted at the rear by No. 31720.

S. C. Nash

This was closed during BR days. The LCDR also had a branch to Ashford (the Maidstone & Ashford Railway) terminating at Ashford LCDR station, a four-platform terminal. Upon amalgamation, the SECR closed the old Ashford LCDR terminus to passengers and diverted trains to Ashford main line station. Thus Maidstone to Ashford is no longer a branch line but a through line and is a useful diversionary route. A similar situation existed at Sevenoaks where the now through route from Sevenoaks via Otford was a LCDR branch from Swanley Junction. The present Ashford to Hastings line is now reduced to single line status from Appledore and this former main line could almost be termed a branch. Tovil Goods in Maidstone closed to all traffic on 3 October 1977.

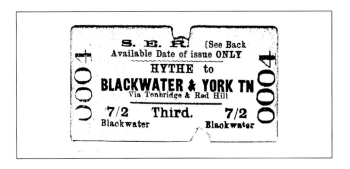

Branch Lines in Surrey and Sussex

Lewes to Seaford (8¾ miles)

The first railway in the area was the LBSCR line to Newhaven Harbour, opened on 8 December 1847 from Lewes. The LBSCR was keen to get a share of the Continental traffic to compete with the South Eastern Railway at Folkestone. The extension from Newhaven on to Seaford was opened on 1 June 1864 and the line was electrified on 1 July 1935. A feature of train working on the line was the operation of the Newhaven boat trains, especially in steam days. When these were run, relief trains in the summer were worked by the LBSCR H2 class 4-4-2s until the class was withdrawn in the 1950s. The normal boat trains were worked in post-war years by the SR electric locomotives BR Nos 20001-20003, known to railway staff as 'Hornbys' on account of their appearance. A visit to Newhaven shed in the 1950s could be very rewarding as all the locomotives on shed would be of LBSCR origin – K class 2-6-0s, E4 class 0-6-2Ts, AIX 0-6-0Ts, and of course the H2 4-4-2s.

Lewes to East Grinstead (Culver Junction-East Grinstead)

The last train ran on the 20¼-mile stretch of line from East Grinstead to Lewes on 16 March 1958 and was hauled by BR Standard Class 4 2-6-4T No. 80154 – the last locomotive built at Brighton. The well-known Bluebell saga began when BR closed the line on 29 May 1955 instead of the proposed 13 June 1955. This was because of the ASLEF strike, but a local resident pointed out that the line had been closed illegally because an Act of Parliament was required to close the line. BR had to reopen the line until the necessary legal proceedings had been dealt with; so the line reopened in 1956 only to close again in 1958. But all was not lost, as this gave time for the preservation bid to be formulated and the line opened again on 7 August 1960 between Horsted Keynes and Sheffield Park as the Bluebell Railway. This was the first preserved standard gauge passenger railway and as a result the line is host to some really old locomotives including two LBSCR AIX class 0-6-0Ts as well as many other now unique Southern types.

The story is not yet complete, for the Bluebell is working towards reopening the line through to East Grinstead from the present terminal site at Kingscote. The process is very lengthy, as land has to be re-purchased from individuals who bought it from BR after the 1958 closure. In the original act, Barcombe and Kingscote stations were not mentioned so they were not reopened in 1956. The railway was opened by the LBSCR in 1882 and proved to be a useful diversionary route for the London to Brighton main line. The Bluebell has now become an established institution, visited every year by day trippers and tourists and the line has featured many times in films, television advertisements and plays, and nearly everyone recognises the railway the instant it flickers on to the TV screen. Barcombe station is now a house and Newick & Chailey has been built over.

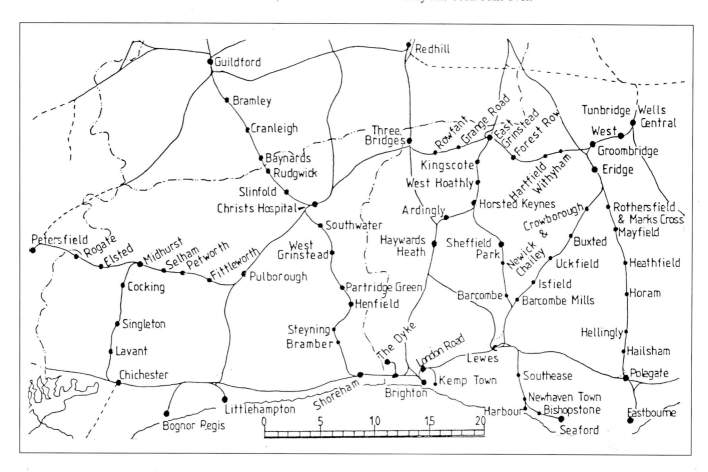

Seaford was opened by the LBSCR on 1 June 1864 but the scene depicted here shows the company's attempt at economy by using petrol railbuses on branch line services. The railway bought two such vehicles in 1905, constructed by Dick, Kerr & Co., but they proved to be unreliable and many years before their time. No. 4 was eventually withdrawn by the SR in 1931 having been used as an inspection saloon from 1911.

East Grinstead Low Level on 20 March 1965 with the ex North London Railway 0-6-0T No. 2650 performing some shunting in the goods yard. This locomotive was loaned by the Bluebell Railway to the contractors for demolition work on the line from Horsted Keynes to East Grinstead.

S. C. Nash

West Hoathly station in Southern Railway days looking towards Horsted Keynes. The station was in Sharpthorne, the village of West Hoathly being farther afield. The building has been demolished and only the platform edges survive today. The war time white painted stripes are visible on the posts in this view.

L&GRP

Horsted Keynes on 18 August 1934 when the spot was a rural backwater of the Southern system. The D1 0-4-2T, No. 2221, is about to work a railmotor set to Haywards Heath. The engine was built at Brighton as No. 221 *Warbleton* in June 1885 and withdrawn in 1940.

H. F. Wheeller

Horsted Keynes on 16 April 1955, with a K class 2-6-0 No. 32342 on the 3.28pm Haywards Heath to London Bridge. The Lewes service was withdrawn on 29 May 1955, from what was to become the Bluebell Railway. The K class Moguls dated from 1913 and were all withdrawn by the end of 1962, with no member of the class having been preserved.

S. C. Nash

The last train from Lewes to East Grinstead on 16 March 1958 is seen at Horsted Keynes, headed by Class 4 2-6-4T No. 80154 – the last engine to be built at Brighton Works. The lower quadrant signals were of pre-Grouping origin and made a fine backdrop to the scene but photographers had to be careful as the line from Haywards Heath was electrified!

M7 class No. 30053 masquerading as No. 30124 is seen on the Bluebell on 18 February 1994 on a Silcock special near Freshfield. The Bulleid stock in Southern green gives the impression of a branch line train of the 1960s but all is not what it seems!

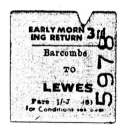

Sheffield Park on 25 August 1934 with E5 class 0-6-2T No. 2573 taking water whilst heading a 'birdcage' set on a train for Victoria. The engine was built at Brighton as No. 573 *Nutbourne* in 1903 and withdrawn by BR in July 1953. The signal box was removed shortly afterwards and an open frame provided on the down platform.

H. F. Wheeller

Sheffield Park station on 15 March 1958, just prior to closure of the line for the second time. The line opened on 1 August 1882 originally and reopened as the Bluebell Railway on 7 August 1960. The scene here has changed greatly as the station is now the thriving centre of what was the country's first preserved standard gauge passenger railway.

CLOSING OF EAST GRINSTEAD-LEWES LINE

On and from MONDAY, 17th MARCH, 1958, the passenger service on the line between EAST GRINSTEAD and LEWES, via SHEFFIELD PARK, will be withdrawn and the following stations closed:—

WEST HOATHLY
SHEFFIELD PARK
NEWICK & CHAILEY

HORSTED KEYNES will remain open for passenger and freight traffic, and be served by trains to and from HAYWARDS HEATH.

'Bus facilities in the area are provided by Southdown Motor Services Ltd.

SOUTHERN

Last days of the Lewes to East Grinstead line, as seen from the road bridge at Newick & Chailey. Class 4 2-6-4T No. 80011 clanks out for East Grinstead in March 1958 with a train of Maunsell stock.

Newick & Chailey station with Class 4 2-6-4T No. 80011 and Miss Bessemer on the platform, right. It was Miss Bessemer who pointed out that the line had been closed illegally in 1955 which eventually forced BR to reopen the line in 1956, thus giving sufficient time for the preservation bid to get underway. Newick & Chailey station site has since been built over.

Haywards Heath to Horsted Keynes (4¾ miles)

This line connected with the Bluebell at Horsted Keynes, a remote junction in the depths of Sussex having been opened by the LBSCR on 3 September 1883. The line was electrified in 1935 and provided with a service from Seaford which was intended to run to East Grinstead eventually, as an electrified through route. However, the 1939-1945 war stopped all that and Horsted Keynes was left high and dry as an odd backwater with an electric branch until the line closed to all traffic on 28 March 1963 but the stub end of the branch to Ardingly ARC stone terminal is still in use for freight trains. For modern day visitors wishing to sample the past, a visit to the refreshment room at the Bluebell Railway's Horsted Keynes station is recommended.

Three Bridges to East Grinstead

Opened on 9 July 1855 this was the first railway to East Grinstead, running for a distance of 6¾ miles. The High Level and extensions east and south from East Grinstead were completed in 1884. There were two intermediate stations on the line – one at Grange Road and the other at Rowfant, which is still in situ. The line was dieselised after 1965 and lasted until 2 January 1967 when it was closed to all traffic. Most of

the line is now a public footpath and bridleway known as the Worth Way. The High Level at East Grinstead was dismantled in 1970 leaving East Grinstead Low Level as the station in use today on the present line from South Croydon which was electrified in 1987.

Horsham to Guildford (19½ miles)

The single track line from Christ's Hospital to Guildford (Peasmarsh Junction) was opened throughout on 2 October 1865. There were intermediate stations at Slinfold, Rudgwick, Baynards, Cranleigh and Bramley. Christ's Hospital as a station was not opened until 28 April 1902, with the re-siting of the school of that name. The branch was just outside the London suburban area and retained a rural appearance about it right up until closure on 14 June 1965. Had the line been electrified it would probably still be open. Most of the trackbed is now a public footpath and bridleway, the stations having been demolished except Baynards, which has been restored to its original condition by its owner – a devoted enthusiast. The remains of the platforms at Bramley can still be seen where the SR concrete nameboard is still in position – Bramley & Wonersh. Closure of this line could have been a short-sighted policy as new housing estates have sprung up

Ardingly in the last days of the passenger services, on 26 March 1963, with a four-car train consisting of 2 BIL stock approaching. The spacious LBSCR buildings have now been demolished but the line survives today as it is used for ARC stone trains. The line was opened on 2 September 1883 and closed by BR on 28th March 1963.

Another view of Ardingly on 26 March 1963 with a Horsted Keynes to Haywards Heath train consisting of two 2 BIL units, with set No. 2624 leading. The line from Horsted Keynes was a useful diversionary route when the main line was blocked for any reason.

Rowfant in the snow with M7 No. 30053 about to propel the train to Three Bridges on 23 February 1963. The line opened for traffic on 9 July 1855 and lasted until 2 January 1967. The engine has survived and is one of the two M7 class 0-4-4Ts in preservation.

Grange Road station on the Three Bridges to East Grinstead line with ex LSWR M7 class 0-4-4T No. 30055 belting away with the 1.8pm from Three Bridges. The site has changed considerably since this 1963 photograph was taken as the station has been demolished and a housing development occupies the site. The Worth Way, a public footpath, now runs most of the way from East Grinstead to Three Bridges.

S. C. Nash

Grange Road on 16 March 1958 with ex SECR H class 0-4-4T No. 31530 about to propel a former LBSCR two-coach push-and-pull set to East Grinstead.

Christ's Hospital was the junction for the Guildford branch and M7 class 0-4-4T No. 30048 is seen arriving here with the 12.21pm Horsham to Guildford on 3 August 1953. A Southern PMV van heads an LBSCR two-coach railmotor set.
S. C. Nash

Slinfold was a quiet backwater on the Christ's Hospital to Guildford branch which closed to all traffic on 14 June 1965. Ivatt 2-6-2T No. 41294 is seen leaving on a Horsham train on 5 June 1965, just a few days before the closure.

Rudgwick on the Guildford to Horsham branch on 10 June 1965 with Ivatt 2-6-2T No. 41299 waiting with a Bulleid three-coach set. The station has been demolished and the site built upon, but the Downs Link footpath runs through on the old trackbed.

Baynards was a classic spot and remotely situated. Behind the LBSCR signal box can be seen the famous dahlia beds for which the station was famous. The station has been preserved and restored to the 'Brighton' livery of chocolate and cream.

Cranleigh station with an H class No. 31279, waiting to cross on 8 August 1959. This 0-4-4T was built at Ashford in November 1909 and scrapped a month after the photograph was taken in September 1959. This idyllic scene has been erased as the buildings have been demolished and the site is now occupied by a car park.

No. 31279 blows off impatiently at Cranleigh as another member of the H class, No. 31543, runs in from Guildford with a three-coach set consisting of ex SECR coaches. The latter engine was built at Ashford in 1909 for the SECR and withdrawn by BR in July 1963.

Bramley & Wonersh with Ivatt 2-6-2T No. 41287 running in from Guildford on 5 June 1965. The signal box has a passenger walkway underneath it so that people can get to the platform. The platform survives today as well as the concrete nameboard. The site is on the Downs Link walk.

along the route. Most of the route of this former branch is now known as the Downs Link walk.

Crowhurst to Bexhill West
This 4½-mile branch was opened by the SECR on 1 June 1902, giving a much shorter journey for passengers to London of 62 miles as against 78 via the LBSCR route. The line was closed during World War I from 1 January 1917 until reopened on 1 March 1919. The station buildings at Bexhill were on a grand scale and the exterior facade was in a fine late-Victorian style. The branch was dieselised in June 1958 but closed completely on 15 June 1964. Had the main line from Tunbridge Wells to Hastings been electrified in 1961 with the rest of the South Eastern Division lines, the branch may have remained open. The station buildings at Bexhill still survive.

Tunbridge Wells West to Groombridge and Eridge
Tunbridge Wells West closed to all traffic on 12 August 1985, with the passenger service from Eridge having ceased on 8 July that year. Tunbridge Wells Central station was renamed Tunbridge Wells on 30 September 1985. Built by the SECR in 1911 it was renovated for the complete Hastings line electrification scheme. Tunbridge Wells West station is now a

Beefeater Restaurant with the former yard and station site now being occupied by a Sainsburys supermarket and car park. A newly constructed platform exists next door to the old engine shed for the Spa Valley Railway which commenced operations of a steam service in December 1996 as the first step towards reopening through to Eridge. Groombridge station is now used as offices where the track has been diverted away from the platform and around some new houses built on the original trackbed. A new platform has been built to the west of the road bridge in anticipation of the reinstatment of steam hauled trains.

Tunbridge Wells to East Grinstead
The 13½-mile East Grinstead to Tunbridge Wells line opened on 1 October 1866 with intermediate stations at Forest Row, Hartfield, Withyham and Groombridge. The line was later to cross the line from Oxted to Eridge, constructed at a later date. The East Grinstead to Ashurst Junction section closed to all traffic on 2 January 1967. The connecting line, Ashurst Junction to Groombridge, closed to all traffic on 6 January 1969. Forest Row station was built over after closure but Hartfield and Withyham are still intact and in a fine state of repair having been sold by BR. The former is in use as a children's nursery and the latter as a private house. Today, the

Bramley & Wonersh in its final years of operation was a crossing point and boasted a W. H. Smith's bookstall built in to the station house. Photographed in June 1965.

A wintry scene at Partridge Green as M7 class 0-4-4T No. 30055 propels out with a three-coach set past the LBSCR starting signal in January 1959. The LBSCR oil lamps are about to be lit up on the down platform.

M7 class No. 30055 leaves Steyning with a three-coach set on 3 January 1959. The line was opened in 1861 and closed to passengers on 7 March 1966. The site is now occupied by the town by-pass.

Christ's Hospital on 22 March 1958 with M7 class 0-4-4T No. 30049 easing out of the down platform with a three-coach set bound for Brighton via the Steyning line. No. 30049 was built at the LSWR's Nine Elms Works in 1905 and was transferred to the Central Division by BR to replace older Brighton types. The station at Christ's Hospital was opened in 1902 by the LBSCR but the buildings were demolished in 1972.

West Grinstead station with E4 class 0-6-2T No. 32468 on the 1.30pm Brighton to Horsham on 7 October 1961, the occasion of the centenary of the Steyning line. The engine was built as No. 468 *Midhurst* in 1898 and survived until January 1963.

S. C. Nash

West Grinstead in May 1962 with an Ivatt Class 2 2-6-2T arriving with a Brighton train. The line was closed to all traffic on 7 March 1966, from Itchingfield Junction to Beeding. Most of the line is now the Downs Link walk.

Bexhill West in 1962, showing the dilapidated roof of the former SECR showpiece station, the frontage of which still exists. The branch was opened on 1 June 1902 to rival the alternative LBSCR route which still survives. This line was closed by BR on 15 June 1964 and the station buildings are now in use as Gorringes Auction Galleries.

G. Daniels

Bexhill West on 30 March 1957, with Wainright H class No. 31520 at rest. Built at Ashford in 1909, the engine lasted until August 1960 having been converted for push-and-pull working in June 1949.

J. R. Langford

Bexhill West with D class No. 31092 about to depart with the 7.2pm to Tonbridge on 4 June 1950. The 4-4-0 was built by Dübs & Co. in March 1903 for the SECR and withdrawn in June 1951 by BR. The grubby engine has a train of Maunsell stock, the leading vehicle of which is in the BR red and cream livery of the 1948 to 1956 period.

S. C. Nash

The most noticeable engineering feature on the Bexhill West branch was the massive brick viaduct at Sidley, now demolished. The C class 0-6-0 and 'birdcage' three-coach set are completely dwarfed by the structure in this January 1952 view.

S. C. Nash

Tunbridge Wells West with Bulleid Pacific No. 34066 *Spitfire* heading an RCTS/LCGB special on 22 March 1964. The station buildings in the background have survived as a Beefeater restaurant and the engine shed is now the headquarters of the Spa Valley Railway. The goods shed and carriage sidings have made way for a supermarket car park.

Hugh Ballantyne

N class 2-6-0 No. 31400 is seen leaving Grove Tunnel on 15 May 1964 with the 11.45am Eastbourne to Tonbridge. The engine was built in July 1932 at Ashford, but was withdrawn a month after this photograph was taken.

S. C. Nash

Groombridge with C2X class 0-6-0 No. 32529 double-heading with an I3 class 4-4-2T, No. 32090 on 14 October 1950. The train is the 1.8pm Tunbridge Wells West to London Bridge via East Grinstead. The I3 did not have long to go as it was withdrawn from service the following month.
S. C. Nash

Hartfield station on the Tunbridge Wells to East Grinstead line with M7 class No. 30055, seen here propelling the 5.8pm from Three Bridges on 17 May 1963. The line was closed to all traffic on 2 January 1967 having been opened by the LBSCR on 1 October 1866. Hartfield station today survives as a children's nursery with the Southern green enamel signs outside the building.

SECR E class 4-4-0 No. 31176 blows off as it climbs to Crowborough from Redgate Mill Junction with the 11.8am Tonbridge to Brighton on 20 August 1951. This engine was built at Ashford in 1907 and was withdrawn shortly after the photograph was taken.

S. C. Nash

A pre-Grouping type scene is depicted here as E5 class 0-6-2T No. 32404 passes Redgate Mill Junction signal box on 11 June 1951. The signalman is offering the staff to the crew of the engine of the 7pm Tunbridge Wells West to Eastbourne. The engine started out life as No. 404 *Hardham* in 1904 on the LBSCR and was withdrawn in 1951.

S. C. Nash

route of the line is walkable from Groombridge to East Grinstead along a footpath known as the Forest Way. The section in the cutting at East Grinstead has been turned into a road bypass as part of the A22, and is known as Beeching Way – named after a well-known local resident who had railway connections.

Tunbridge Wells to Lewes

There was an hourly service from Tonbridge to Brighton in BR steam days, usually worked by Tonbridge locomotives. These could be anything from an elderly Wainwright D class 4-4-0 to a Maunsell Mogul. The 24 miles from Tunbridge Wells West to Lewes was the second LBSCR line to open from Tunbridge Wells, the line through Eridge and Uckfield opening for traffic on 3 August 1868. The section from Uckfield to Lewes had been opened on 18 October 1858, the line from the Lewes end having originally left there from the main London line facing northwards. The line was opened as the Lewes & Uckfield Railway and was purchased by the LBSCR in 1864. The old spur from the Uckfield line facing towards Lewes from the main line, was put out of use with the

Tunbridge Wells opening in 1868 but the abandoned line can still be seen, although mainly overgrown. Today, Uckfield is a branch from Hurst Green Junction, the Uckfield to Lewes section having been closed to all traffic on 24 February 1969. In the summer of 1984, a privately operated steam railway was opened at Isfield and runs for a short distance along the old trackbed towards Uckfield. The Lavender Line, as it is known, operates for about half a mile from Isfield but is being extended having changed hands a few years ago. The station has been carefully restored to Southern Railway colours and has all the uasual facilities including a gift shop and refreshment rooms etc. Barcombe Mills is now a restaurant and the terminus station at Uckfield has been resited on the other side of the road to eliminate the level crossing.

Tunbridge Wells to Eastbourne (29¾ miles)

The line from Eridge to Polegate via Heathfield was closed to all traffic by 9 September 1968, the section from Heathfield to Hailsham having closed completely on 26 April 1968. The passenger service from Eridge to Hailsham and the freight

N class 2-6-0 No. 31816 approaches Rotherfield with the 7.27am Redhill to Eastbourne in August 1964. The Mogul was built at Ashford in 1921 and lasted until January 1966. The line survived until 14 June 1965 when the passenger service was withdrawn.

S. C. Nash

A picturesque scene at Argos Hill as BR Standard Class 4 No. 80010 threads the cutting with the 10.30am Tunbridge Wells West to Eastbourne. Most of the 'Cuckoo' line is now a footpath known as the Cuckoo Walk.

S. C. Nash

Crossing at Horam on the former 'Cuckoo' line, Class 4 2-6-4T No. 80141 waits for an Eastbourne to Tunbridge Wells West train on 4 June 1965, a few days before the line was closed. The Class 4 2-6-4Ts were very useful on the former Central Division as they could work bunker first for long distances between terminals.

Two I3 class 4-4-2Ts double-head the 9.55am Eastbourne to Tunbridge Wells West on 3 March 1951 near Horam on the climb to Heathfield. The I3 class, built at Brighton from 1907 to 1913 to the design of D. E. Marsh, lasted until 1952. The two engines here, Nos 32089 and 32030, were both withdrawn in 1951.

S. C. Nash

Marsh Atlantic No. 32421 leaves Hailsham on 17 June 1951 with the 10.12am Sundays only to Eastbourne. The engine is working a 'filling in' turn from Eastbourne to Hailsham and back. The Southern Railway named the six engines of the H2 class in the period 1925-1926 and No. B421, as it was then, became *South Foreland*. It was built at Brighton in 1911 and survived until 1956 when withdrawn by BR.

S. C. Nash

A now-famous engine that is still with us and runs on specials from time to time is No. 34027 *Taw Valley*. The rebuilt Bulleid Pacific is seen here on 31 May 1963 on a 'filling in' turn at Polegate with the 8.16am Eastbourne to Hailsham. The engine would work the night newspaper train from London Bridge to Eastbourne and then do a stint working passenger trains on the 'Cuckoo' line which closed from Hailsham to Polegate on 9 September 1968.

S. C. Nash

service from Eridge to Heathfield was withdrawn on 14 June 1965. This line was known locally as the Cuckoo Line and had all its ex-LBSCR stations intact at the time of passenger closure. The 'Brighton' preferred subways to footbridges and used a lot of timber in its buildings. A feature of some former LBSCR country stations was the platform signal frame provided by the Southern to reduce costs, as can still be seen at Sheffield Park on the Bluebell Railway. Hailsham to Eridge (Redgate Mill Junction) was opened on 1 September 1880, the Polegate to Hailsham section having opened on 14 May 1849. Most of the line is now a public footpath known as the Cuckoo Walk. Traces of some of the stations can still be seen and Hellingly is now a private residence.

The Oxted to Eridge section of double-track 'main line' was opened from Hurst Green Junction to Edenbridge on 2 January 1888 and Edenbridge (Town) to Eridge on 1 October 1888. Thus, the Eridge triangle was complete by 1888, forming an alternative through route from London to Brighton via Oxted and Uckfield. Today, the line is merely the main line from Uckfield to Hurst Green Junction which has now been singled for part of the way.

Horsham (Itchingfield Junction) to Shoreham

The Steyning line was opened throughout on 16 September 1861, from Shoreham to Itchingfield Junction. The distance from Horsham to Shoreham was 20 miles and there were intermediate stations at Bramber, Steyning, Henfield,

Partridge Green, West Grinstead and Southwater. The line was double track throughout and regarded by the LBSCR as more an alternative route to the coast than a branch line. The line escaped electrification by the Southern Railway in the 1930s and was never planned by BR to be electrified. Class D3 0-4-4Ts from Brighton and Horsham sheds were used for many years but eventually gave way to M7 class 0-4-4Ts. These were never popular with Central Diviison loco crews and did not last very long in the area. They were replaced by Ivatt Class 2 2-6-2Ts.

The line was eventually dieselised in May 1964 and was closed to all traffic on 7 March 1966 except for the Shoreham to Beeding section. This was retained for the cement works but was closed on 1 May 1980. Parts of the line have been built upon, and most of the trackbed has now been turned into a public footpath known as the Downs Link except for a part at Steyning which is now the A283 Steyning bypass. Traces of the stations at West Grinstead and Southwater remain but Partridge Green is now an industrial estate.

The Dyke

An unusual line of 3½ miles which left the main line at Aldrington at sea level, and climbed up to the Dyke on the South Downs at 400ft. The line was opened on 1 September 1887 and catered for day trippers from Brighton. Worked by the LBSCR, the line was closed from 1 January 1917 to 26 July 1920, like so many minor lines during that period. The

The Dyke branch was built in 1887 and took day trippers up on to the downs, 3½ miles from Aldrington on the main line. D1 class 0-4-2T No. B214 simmers in the summer sun having completed the climb with a two-coach set of LBSCR stock. The engine was built in 1874 as No. 13 *Pimlico* and renumbered several times to become No. 214 in 1920. The Southern Railway withdrew the locomotive in 1933.

Lens of Sutton

An unusual contraption appeared on the Dyke branch in 1933 when the Southern Railway employed a Sentinel steam railcar, which is seen here basking in the summer sunlight. The SR Sentinels were not deemed to be successful and after a short life were withdrawn.

National Railway Museum

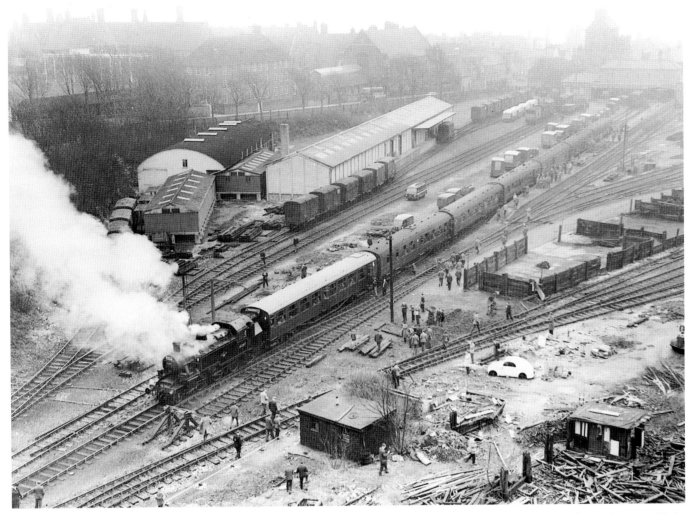

An aerial view of Kemp Town with a Class 2 2-6-2T, No. 41287, on a special in a sea mist. The layout of the station site can be seen with its extensive goods and coal yard. The line closed to passengers on 2 January 1933 and goods on 28 June 1971.

Hugh Ballantyne

line terminated short of the summit which left passengers with another 200ft climb. With the advent of the motorbus, the line's patronage declined. The branch was worked by E4 class 0-6-2Ts at the final closure which took place on 1 January 1939.

Kemp Town

This 1½-mile long suburban line was opened on 2 August 1869. The journey from Kemp Town to Brighton station took 10 minutes and season ticket holders on the main line could travel the branch for no extra charge. The line became operated by push-and-pull trains and was closed temporarily from 1 January 1917 to 1 September 1919. Closure to regular passenger trains took effect from 2 January 1933 but freight train operation lasted much longer and eventually ceased from 28 June 1971. A special service was arranged by BR on Saturday, 26 June 1971 and an hourly service ran between 10.00 and 21.00. Fares were 25p for adults and 15p for children, although the last train of the day cost 50p.

Railways to Midhurst

Midhurst was the centre for three lines, one from Pulborough (11 miles), one from Chichester (12 miles) and the third from Petersfield (9¼ miles). The first two were LBSCR owned whilst the latter was of LSWR origin. Prior to the 1923 Grouping, the LSWR had its own terminal at Midhurst but this was closed on 12 July 1925. The first railway to Midhurst, from Pulborough, was opened on 15 October 1866 and had stations at Fittleworth (1889), Petworth and Selham (1872). The Petersfield line, with intermediate stations at Rogate and Elsted, was opened on 1 September 1864 and worked by the LSWR. The last line to be built to Midhurst was the Chichester branch, opened on 11 July 1881 with stations at Lavant, Singleton and Cocking. This line passed through rural, sparsely populated countryside and saw little traffic, closing to passengers on 6 July 1935. The section of the line from Midhurst to Cocking closed after the branch goods train fell down an embankment on 19 November 1951 near Midhurst, the line having been washed away in a flood. The C2X class 0-6-0 that had worked the train (No. 32522) was retrieved on 25 February 1952 when a special ramp had to be laid in to tow the engine back onto the track. The locomotive was repaired at Brighton Works and remained in service for a further ten years.

The LBSCR station at Midhurst is seen here in 1960 when still complete although the passenger service had been withdrawn in 1955. The station served three lines, one to Pulborough, one to Chicester and another to Petersfield. The station site has since been built on following complete closure in October 1964.

The LSWR had their own station at Midhurst which the Southern closed after the Grouping of 1923. The building can be seen to have survived as a private house in this view dated 25 April 1953 which shows an M7 class 0-4-4T working the 5.2pm Midhurst to Petersfield.

S. C. Nash

The Midhurst to Chichester branch of the former LBSCR had three intermediate stations, at Cocking, Singleton and Lavant. The line opened on 11 July 1881, passed through sparsely populated countryside and closed to passengers on 6 July 1935. Goods trains continued to run after the passenger closure and the official closure date of the Lavant to Cocking section was 31 August 1953. The view here shows a rather dilapidated Singleton station in 1947.

S. C. Nash

Singleton station on the Midhurst to Chichester line has now been converted into a vineyard and winery – a most unusual transformation for a railway station. The station at Cocking is now a private house and the building at Lavant has been converted into flats.

Sketch by T. Willard

Petworth was the original terminus of the line from Hardham Junction. D3 class 0-4-4T No. 2366 can be seen here with a two-coach motor train for Pulborough on 6 August 1934.

H. F. Wheeller

Final days at Petworth as an E4 class 0-6-2T returns from Midhurst with the goods on 14 April 1960. No. 32469 was built at Brighton in June 1898 as No. 469 *Beachy Head* and survived until October 1961. The branch closed to all traffic on 23 May 1966 from Petworth to Pulborough.

E4 class No. 32469 blows off whilst shunting at Petworth on the former LBSCR branch to Midhurst. The station nameboard is still in position in this 1960 view where the station buildings, as well as the railway cottages, have survived as private houses.

M7 class 0-4-4T No. 30328 is seen leaving Selham with a Petersfield to Pulborough train on 15 October 1950. The station still exists although in a dilapidated state.

S. C. Nash

Q class 0-6-0 No. 30531 heads a ramblers' excursion away from Selham on 15 October 1950 with a train of ten Maunsell coaches. Today, even ramblers are carbound to their starting point.

S. C. Nash

Rogate, on the former Midhurst to Petersfield line, is seen here in April 1953. The station survives today but the building is in a very run down state of repair. The line closed to all traffic on 7 February 1955.

S. C. Nash

Petersfield on 4 December 1954 with M7 class 0-4-4T No. 30028 in the single platform bay shortly before the branch closed to all traffic on 7 February 1955. The branch platform has since been demolished.

S. C. Nash

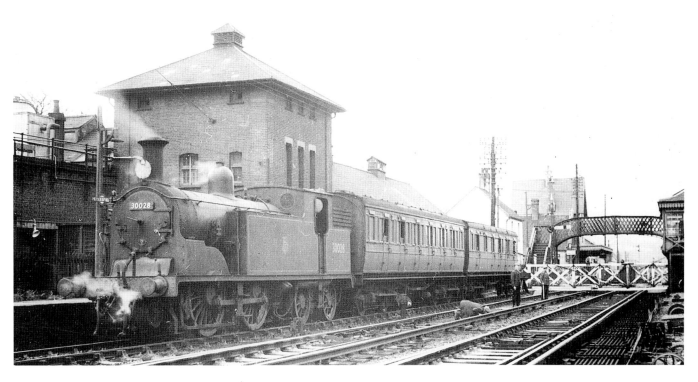

Elstead was one of the two intermediate stations on the former LSWR line from Petersfield to Midhurst. M7 class No. 30047 is seen on 18 June 1951 with a two-coach push-and-pull unit en route to Midhurst where the LSWR had their own station. The site is now an industrial estate.

H. F. Wheeller

The truncated line beyond Lavant to Cocking and Singleton closed to all traffic on 31 August 1953. Part of the Lavant to Chichester line is now a footpath. The stations on the line still survive – one of them, Singleton, is now the Chilsdown Vineyard. All services on the Petersfield to Midhurst line ceased on 7 February 1955, as did the passenger services for Midhurst to Pulborough. Freight traffic ceased from Midhurst to Petworth on 12 October 1964, and Petworth to Pulborough on 23 May 1966. Rogate station survives in a dilapidated state whilst the site of Elsted is an industrial estate. The old LBSCR station at Midhurst has been built over but the LSWR station survives. Petworth and Fittleworth are now houses but Selham is dilapidated.

Miscellaneous lines
The LBSCR did have lines to Bognor Regis, opened 1 June 1864, and Littlehampton, opened 16 March 1846, but as they have through services to London, Brighton and Portsmouth, they cannot be counted as branch lines in the true sense. Chichester was where the West Sussex Railway, or Hundred of Manhood & Selsey Tramway, commenced. The line was 7½ miles long and opened in 1897 as a light railway and was part of the Colonel Stephens empire, closing to all traffic on 19 January 1935. The line was not taken over by the Southern Railway and closed too early to be part of the Southern Region. Had the line survived until 1948, it would have probably been nationalised and disposed of quickly, as with the East Kent Light Railway. The 1½-mile branch of the former South Eastern Railway, from Rye to Rye Harbour, closed on 29 February 1960 and was a goods only line. Part of the route is now a road.

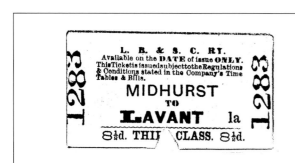

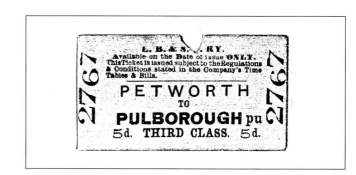

Branch Lines in Hampshire

Farnham to Ash Junction (Surrey)

The short line from Farnham to Ash Junction of less than 3 miles in length had two stations, one at Tongham and the other at Ash Green. The service was from Farnham to Guildford, avoiding Aldershot. The passenger service was withdrawn on 4 July 1937 on the occasion of electrification of the Alton line from Woking. Freight services lasted from Tongham to Ash Junction until 2 January 1961. The track from Farnham Junction to Tongham was lifted in January 1955, the exact date of the cessation of freight trains being unclear. Tongham has been built over but Ash Green remains as a private house. The platform edges survive and a public footpath runs along the old trackbed.

Bentley to Bordon

This line was opened on 11 December 1905 by the LSWR and was a light railway of 4½ miles length. The line was built to connect with the Longmoor Military Railway at Bordon, opened at about the same time. The Longmoor Military Railway had access to its own system from both Bordon and Liss, the LMR having a considerable system where Army engineers were trained. The Longmoor Military Railway had workshops, engine sheds, breakdown cranes and a large garrison. Locomotives and rolling stock were secondhand from the main line railways and the system was very busy during both wars. The platforms at Bordon were sufficiently lengthy to contain troop trains. The Bordon to Bentley branch was worked by LSWR M7 class 0-4-4Ts but closed to passengers on 16 September 1957. Freight traffic ceased on 4 April 1966 and the Longmoor Military Railway closed on 31 October 1969. Some rolling stock survived and the most famous of the Longmoor engines, the blue-liveried 2-10-0 *Gordon*, can now be seen on the Severn Valley Railway. A feature of the Bordon to Bentley branch was the halt at Kingsley where the LSWR planted trees to give some shelter to waiting passengers. The halt has been demolished and Bordon station site covered over by an industrial estate.

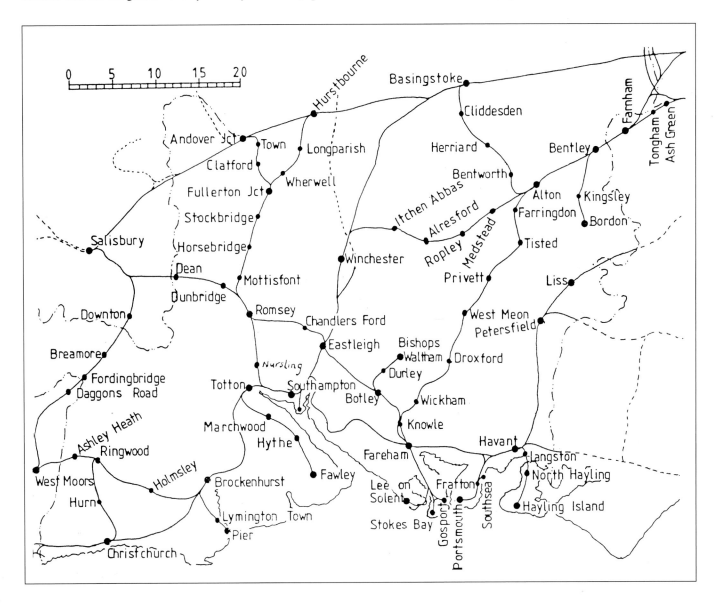

The Tongham branch leaves the main line at Ash Junction with an elderly South Eastern 4-4-0 bound for Reading in Southern Railway days. The B1 class were reboilered by Wainwright, No. 1443 having been built as a B class by Neilson & Co. in 1898. A few survived into the BR era.

Lens of Sutton

Tongham on 26 September 1953 with a railtour special organised by the Enthusiasts Club, later to become the Railway Enthusiasts Club. The engine, No. 30434, was built in 1905 as an L12 class 4-4-0 to the design of Dugald Drummond of the LSWR. The line was closed to passengers in 1937 and freight in 1961. The station at Tongham has disappeared but Ash Green has been well restored and is now a private house. A footpath runs over most of the old trackbed.

S. C. Nash

Bordon station on 14 September 1957 with M7 class 0-4-4T No. 30110 of 1904 waiting to propel to Bentley with an LSWR push-and-pull set. The branch closed to passengers the same weekend but freight traffic lasted until 4 April 1966. The site is now an industrial estate.

S. C. Nash

Kingsley Halt was the only intermediate stopping point on the 4½ mile branch to Bordon. M7 class 0-4-4T No. 30109 is seen here leaving for Bordon, crossing the ungated road with cattle grids. The site has changed but the tree on the left survives.

Hugh Ballantyne

Cliddesden on the occasion of the opening of the line in 1901 with O2 class 0-4-4T No. 203 of 1891 built at Nine Elms. The Basingstoke & Alton Light Railway had a chequered career and closed on 30 December 1916 to be reopened by the Southern on 18 August 1924 and closed again on 12 September 1932.

Lens of Sutton

Alton to Basingstoke

The Basingstoke & Alton Light Railway had a chequered career and a certain amount of fame but little remains to be seen of this interesting line today. The 12½-mile line was opened by the LSWR in 1901 and closed on 30 December 1916 as a wartime economy measure. The Southern Railway reluctantly reopened the line on 18 August 1924 and closed it again on 12 September 1932. The railway had been put there in the first place mainly to keep the GWR from encroaching on South Western territory.

The Southern Railway hired the line out to film companies, the most spectacular film being The Wrecker made in 1928 which featured a South Eastern Railway F1 class 4-4-0 No. A148. The Southern Railway did the thing in style, the *Southern Railway Magazine* reporting the matter in great detail. A special train left Waterloo at 6.30am on Sunday, 19 August 1928 with dining cars full of press photographers and reporters with breakfast being served on the train which terminated at Herriard. The crash was staged at Salters Ash Crossing where the No. A148 with six coaches was crashed into a stationary Foden steam lorry. A large marquee was erected in the field overlooking the crossing and tickets were issued to visitors to see the show from Lasham Hill Farm. The line was used again for filming

purposes in June 1937 when Oh! Mr. Porter was filmed at Cliddesden – one of the most famous of railway films. The Basingstoke & Alton was lifted shortly afterwards but the numberplates and builder's plate of *Northiam*, one of the locomotives used, are still in existence and are at the National Railway Museum, York.

Alton to Winchester

Alton to Alresford is now open to regular passenger trains, being part of the preserved Mid-Hants Railway Watercress Line – a distance of 10½ miles. The Mid-Hants Railway commenced services into Alton from Medstead on 25 May 1985, the track having been reinstated in parts. The section from Ropley to Medstead opened on 28 May 1983, while Alresford to Ropley had been opened on 30 April 1977. The line has a good selection of motive power to greet the visitor, including Bulleid Pacifics, Maunsell Moguls and BR Standard classes. The gradients are fairly tough, so big engines are required to work the trains. The line from Alton to Winchester Junction closed on 5 February 1973, and the section west from Alresford has not been reopened. Itchen Abbas is now a housing development with the station cottages incorporated into the estate. Look for a house called Beeching!

The changing fortunes of Cliddesden on the Basingstoke & Alton Light Railway can be seen here. The top illustration shows the station after the opening of 1901 where a few of the local residents have turned out to be photographed. The platform is made of concrete and the rails are double-ended bull head with wooden keys. The lower picture shows the same spot in 1958 where the site has become overgrown. The concrete platform edges survive but the trees have certainly grown.

Upper photograph by Lens of Sutton

Bentworth & Lasham on the one-time Basingstoke & Alton Light Railway was still complete in 1958 except for the track. The passenger service was withdrawn by the economy-minded Southern Railway on 12 September 1932 and was the terminus of the line until the SR abandoned the track in 1939. The line was used in 1937 for the filming of 'Oh! Mr. Porter', near Cliddesden.

A more recent view of Bentworth & Lasham, taken 19 March 1997, shows that the platform and station building still survive, some 65 years after closure! The scene is little changed from 1958 and the site is still used by the local coal merchant. The tin shack station served as a booking office and waiting room during the railway's heyday.

Herriard on the Basingstoke & Alton Light Railway was a passing place on that short-lived railway which was opened mainly as a blocking line to keep the GWR out of Alton and Southampton.

Lens of Sutton

Ropley station in Southern Railways days with LSWR 0-4-4T No. 8 running in with a train of LSWR stock. The engine was an Adams T1 class built at Nine Elms in 1894. The topiary has been preserved by the Mid-Hants Railway and can be seen today.

A private special hauled by 'West Country' class No. 34010 *Sidmouth* heads for Alresford with a train of Pullmans near Butts Junction on 19 May 1959. The train was for a wedding, (the daughter of Sir Anthony Doughty-Titchborne Bart) and was the only Pullman train to use the line except for the occasionally diverted 'Bournemouth Belle'.

S. C. Nash

Alresford, with snowplough-fitted M7 class 0-4-4T No. 30479 of 1911 and LSWR stock departing for Alton on what is now the 'Watercress Line'. The line was closed by BR on 5 February 1973 reopened by the Mid-Hants Railway to Ropley on 20 April 1977 and subsequently extended back to Alton.

Hugh Ballantyne

Alresford station shortly after dieselisation by the Southern Region on 18 May 1958. Diesel electric multiple unit set No. 1114 arrives on a down working. The station is now the western terminus of the 'Watercress Line' which opened right through to Alton on 25 May 1985. The section on to Winchester Junction closed by BR on 5 February 1973, was abandoned and the track lifted.

Hurstbourne to Fullerton Junction was opened by the LSWR on 1 June 1885 with two intermediate stations, one at Longparish and the other at Wherwell. Longparish station, seen here on 30 October 1957, was closed to passengers on 6 July 1931 and freight on 28 May 1956. It is now a very well restored private residence.

S. C. Nash

Hurstbourne to Fullerton Junction

This 7½-mile connecting line from Hurstbourne on the main West of England line was opened on 1 June 1885, to Fullerton Junction on the LSWR Andover Junction to Romsey branch. This was built as a double-track line with the intention of keeping the GWR out of Southampton. A spur was planned and was even been partially built from the GWR, Newbury to Winchester line near Whitchurch. The intermediate stations were at Longparish and Wherwell and were intact when the line closed completely on 28 May 1956. The Hurstbourne to Longparish section had been closed to all traffic in 1934, the passenger service ceasing on 6 July 1931. Longparish and Wherwell stations still exist and are in use as private residences.

Brockenhurst-Bournemouth (via Wimborne) and Christchurch

This was the original route to Christchurch and Bournemouth prior to the opening of the more direct main line through New Milton. The line to Christchurch went via Ringwood and

Hurn (5½ miles) and lasted until 30 September 1935, having been opened on 13 November 1862. The Brockenhurst-Ringwood-Dorchester main line was opened on 1 June 1847. The 22¾-mile route from Brockenhurst to Broadstone Junction was useful to the Southern when running diversions avoiding Bournemouth. In the summer timetable certain Waterloo to Weymouth trains ran via Ringwood on Saturdays. The standard service in BR days, usually an M7 class 0-4-4T on a push-and-pull set, was worked from Bournemouth West to Brockenhurst. The line closed to all traffic on 4 May 1964 from Brockenhurst to Ringwood, and on 7 August 1967 from Ringwood to West Moors. The original 'main line' from Ringwood to Christchurch had one intermediate station at Hurn and, although this was closed in September 1935, the station can still be visited as it is now the Avon Causeway Hotel (pub and restaurant). The track was lifted in 1937. Holmsley is now The Old Station Tearooms with the trackbed forming a road. Ringwood station site is now a road and Wimborne an industrial estate. Some parts of the line have been converted to footpaths.

Wherwell station on 30 October 1957, a year after complete closure, looking towards Fullerton Junction. The passenger service had ceased on 6 July 1931. The line was built by the LSWR to keep the GWR out of the area. The station is now a private residence in a housing development.

S. C. Nash

Fullerton Junction on 17 August 1955 with a grubby 700 class 0-6-0, No. 30306, on the goods from Longparish, which ceased with the closure of the line on 28 May 1956. The junction ceased to function after the Andover Junction to Romsey line closed on 7 September 1964. A Mogul can be seen shunting in the yard behind the waiting passengers. The station houses are still in situ as private residences and part of the platform remains.

J. H. Aston

A T9 class 4-4-0 leaves Fullerton Junction on 2 November 1957 bound for Southampton from Andover Junction, just prior to dieselisation. No. 30284 was built at Nine Elms in November 1899 and heads a Bulleid three-coach set. The former Longparish branch can be seen on the right.

T9 No. 30287 of 1900 is seen drifting into Fullerton Junction on 2 November 1957 with the 12.53pm Portsmouth to Andover Junction. The train consists of BR standard stock in the old red and cream livery. The line closed to all traffic on 7 September 1964.

S. C. Nash

Holmsley station on 18 May 1963 with M7 class No. 30108 about to propel out for Brockenhurst. The line from Brockenhurst to Dorchester was opened on 1 June 1847 and Holmsley, in the heart of the New Forest, was the first station out from the junction. The station survives as the Old Station Tea Rooms and the trackbed is now a road.

Ringwood with Bournemouth M7 No. 30108 again, with Maunsell stock on 18 May 1963. The passenger service was withdrawn by BR on 4 May 1964, the section from Brockenhurst being to all traffic. The Ringwood to West Moors line was closed to freight traffic on 7 August 1967 and the station site at Ringwood is now occupied by a road.

A Bournemouth to Brockenhurst train hauled by M7 class 0-4-4T No. 30379 waits time on 18 May 1963, a year before the service was withdrawn. The buildings have been demolished and the trackbed turned into a road and a roundabout now exists on the site of the crossing gates.

Andover Junction to Romsey

The Andover & Redbridge Railway opened on 6 March 1865 making a connection with the main line through to Southampton. The railway was independent and was built on the course of the Andover Canal. The LSWR acquired the Andover & Redbridge and extended the line from Andover Town to Andover Junction on the main line. The Midland & South Western Junction Railway connected with the LSWR at Andover Junction, and as a result, through services ran from the north of England to Southampton. The through services continued up until closure of the M&SWJR on 11 September 1961 when that line was closed. There had been through trains from Cheltenham to Southampton and Southern Region engines had worked them right through to Cheltenham. The 18-mile Andover Junction to Romsey line closed to all traffic on 7 September 1964, but the section from Andover Town to Andover Junction lasted until 18 September 1967 for freight.

The loss of the through route from the North was the primary cause of the Andover to Romsey line's eclipse. The line was dieselised in 1958, prior to which it was worked by T9 class 4-4-0s of LSWR origin. There are proposals to convert Andover to Romsey into a continuous walk with some parts already being public footpaths or highways. Andover Town, Clatford and Stockbridge stations have disappeared but Fullerton and Mottisfont are now houses. Horsebridge station has been fully restored, complete with a 1921 LSWR carriage converted into a camping coach.

Alton to Fareham (Meon Valley Railway)

The Meon Valley line, 22¼ miles in length, was opened on

1 June 1903 by the LSWR and was intended as an alternative main line to Fareham and Portsmouth. The line was opened fairly late for a main line, for the LSWR was wary of the GWR who always had ambitions to expand to the coast in the Solent area. There were stations at Tisted, Privett, West Meon, Droxford and Wickham, some of which still exist having been turned into private houses. Halts were opened at Farringdon (1931) and Knowle (1907). The station buildings were unusual in that they had sliding doors on the platform entrance from the booking hall. A peculiarity of the route was the section which was opened in 1904 by the LSWR who built a double-track deviation line from Knowle Junction into Fareham around Knowle Tunnel. The single-track section through Knowle Tunnel was still used by Meon Valley trains until closure. The passenger service was withdrawn on 7 February 1955 and the section from Droxford to Farringdon closed to all traffic on the same day. The stub end of the line from Farringdon to Alton survived until 5 August 1968. At the bottom end of the line services ceased for all traffic from Knowle Junction to Droxford on 30 April 1962. The station at Droxford was used for the HQ of the Allied Expeditionary Force in 1944 and was where the Prime Minister's train was stabled in the sidings. A framed photograph of Churchill and Eisenhower used to hang in the booking hall at this station. The Meon Valley line was railtoured on 6 February 1955 by an RCTS special headed by two T9 class 4-4-0s, Nos 30301 and 30732. The Meon Valley was worked by many of the LSWR locomotive types up to closure, including M7 class 0-4-4 tanks on the push-and-pull, 700 class 0-6-0s on the goods, and T9 class 4-4-0s on the occasional through train.

The Romsey to Andover Junction line, known facetiously as the 'sprat & winkle' because most of it was built over a canal, came close to the main road near Fullerton where T9 class 4-4-0 No. 30284 is seen heading north on 1 November 1957.

Mottisfont station on the Andover Junction to Romsey line is seen on 2 November 1957 with T9 class 4-4-0 No. 30732 of 1900. The station house is still in existence although the site is very overgrown today. Note the oil lamps for station lighting.

The Meon Valley line was opened as late as 1 June 1903 by the LSWR and ran through picturesque countryside. L12 class 4-4-0 No. 30420 of 1904 is seen on a pick up goods in 1949. The L12 class of 20 engines were built from 1904 to 1905 to the design of Dugald Drummond. The train is near West Meon where the station has disappeared but a footpath now runs to Knowle.

E. C. Griffith

Droxford on the occasion of a Branch Line Society special on 7 March 1959 with M7 class No. 30111. The passenger service was withdrawn on 7 February 1955 but the line to Droxford survived until 30 April 1962. The station is now a well-restored private residence.

Wickham on the Meon Valley line with the BLS special on 7 March 1959, then still open for freight traffic. Although the line to Droxford closed in April 1962 the Farringdon to Alton section lasted until 5 August 1968. M7 class 0-4-4T No. 30111, a Bournemouth engine at the time, was built in 1904. The station has been demolished and the site is completely overgrown but a footpath runs through what is now a wood.

700 class 0-6-0 No. 30698 runs into Alton with a pick up goods from the Meon Valley line, some time before closure of the line to all traffic. The 700 class, known to enginemen as 'black motors', were a Drummond goods engine and dated from 1897. There were 30 in the class which were built by Dübs but all were reboiled by Urie and Maunsell. None survive today.

Hugh Ballantyne

Today, Tisted, Privett and Droxford survive as private houses having been beautifully restored. West Meon and Wickham stations have been razed to the ground, but the trackbed from there to Knowle Junction is now a public footpath.

There was a short but abortive attempt at preservation on the Meon Valley. Mr Charles Ashby bought Droxford station and used the track to test the Sadler Pacerailer railbus during the 1960s. The line also had AIX No. 32646 which was stored at Droxford until 1966 when it was sent to Hayling Island to be mounted outside a pub. This 'Terrier' is now at Haven Street on the Isle of Wight Steam Railway. The Southern Loco Preservation Co. bought a diesel shunter and USA tanks Nos 30064 and 30072 in 1969 and then moved to Liss. Eventually, No. 30064 ended up on the Bluebell and No. 30072 on the Keighley & Worth Valley.

Bishops Waltham
This 3½-mile branch from Botley was opened on 6 June 1863 as the Bishops Waltham Railway, and was purchased by the LSWR in 1864. Passenger services ceased at an early date – on 2 January 1933 – but the daily goods lasted until 30 April 1962 when the line was closed completely. There was one intermediate halt at Durley, opened in 1909 for the LSWR

railmotor service. The terminus at Bishops Waltham has been obliterated by a road scheme.

The Southsea Railway (East Southsea Branch)
A 1½-mile long line from Fratton to Southsea, opened on 2 July 1885 and jointly owned by the LBSCR and the LSWR. It was worked by railmotors and closed on 8 August 1914 as a wartime economy measure but never reopened.

Gosport and Lee-on-Solent
The 4¼-mile Gosport branch was one of the LSWR's oldest lines – in fact the line was opened as a main line terminus on 29 November 1841 being a branch off the London & Southampton Railway from Eastleigh (then called Bishopstoke). The line gave access to Portsmouth via Gosport station which had a superb colonnade, but after the opening of Portsmouth Harbour, Gosport station declined in importance. The branch had royal patronage as Queen Victoria used the line to Clarence Pier on her way to the Isle of Wight. The passenger service to Gosport from Fareham ceased on 8 June 1953. The section from Bedenham to Gosport station closed to all traffic on 6 January 1969. The Fareham to Gosport line had a branch to Stokes Bay from Gosport Junction, just

Botley with M7 class No. 30033, built at Nine Elms in 1898, preparing to work the daily goods down the branch to Bishops Waltham on 8 March 1958. The main line from Portsmouth to Eastleigh has since been electrified.

The Bishops Waltham goods has arrived at Botley, hauled by M7 class No. 30033. The LSWR station has oil lamps mounted on posts made form old rails, with the original blue glass bearing the station's name.

Bishops Waltham was the terminus of the 3½-mile branch from Botley opened on 6 June 1863 by the nominally independent Bishops Waltham Railway. Here, M7 class No. 30033 is seen running round the branch goods on 8 March 1958.

Bishops Waltham station still displayed the Southern Railway signs in green and white enamel in 1958. The passenger service was withdrawn on 2 January 1933 but the daily goods continued to run and the line eventually closed to all traffic on 30 April 1962. The site has now been erased by a road scheme.

Gosport station was the original terminus of the London & Southampton Railway and opened in 1841 but the route declined in importance after the opening of the Portsmouth direct line in 1859. The normal passenger service was withdrawn by BR on 9 June 1953 and the freight on 6 January 1969. The remains of the station have been preserved by Hampshire County Council as the colonnade was a listed structure. Today the roofless remains look more like an ancient monument. The BLS railtour stops for photography in 1959.

Fort Brockhurst is seen on the occasion of the BLS outing on 7 March 1959 with M7 class 0-4-4T No. 30111 of 1904 and LSWR push-and-pull set No. 6. The station was the junction for the short-lived Lee-on-Solent branch which was closed in 1931. The station house survives today as a private residence with the old Lee-on-Solent bay platform still extant.

A Lee-on-Solent train departs from Fort Brockhurst on 4 August 1930 with O2 class 0-4-4T No. E232 (built Nine Elms 1895) and an LSWR two-coach set with fold down steps for use at intermediate halts. The branch was opened on 12 May 1894 and closed on 1 January 1931. The station at Lee-on-Solent became an amusement arcade.

H. F. Wheeller

outside Gosport station. The Stokes Bay line and pier were opened on 6 April 1863, worked by the LSWR and sold to the Admiralty on 3 March 1922. The purpose of the line to Stokes Bay was to give a shorter sea crossing to the Isle of Wight, but the regular passenger service finished on 1 November 1915. The Admiralty took over the pier during World War I and used it for torpedo research.

The 3-mile Lee-on-Solent Light Railway opened in 1894 from Fort Brockhurst – an intermediate station on the Gosport branch. Freight services ceased on 29 September 1935, the passenger service having been withdrawn on 1 January 1931. The disused section from Fareham to Bedenham near Gosport is still in situ and the old trackbeds to Stokes Bay and Fort Brockhurst are now public footpaths. The LSWR used ex-LBSCR AIX class 0-6-0Ts on the railmotor to Lee-on-Solent and Bishops Waltham. These engines were purchased by the LSWR in 1903 and numbered 734 and 735. No 734 (ex-LBSCR No. 46) survived until November 1963, having worked the Hayling Island branch until closure. This was the locomotive, mentioned previously, which had worked on the Isle of Wight and was mounted on a plinth outside a pub at Hayling but is now once again on the Isle of Wight. Gosport station, or the remains of it, have been beautifully restored by Hampshire County Council. Lee-on-Solent station is now an amusement arcade and Fort Brockhurst station survives as a private residence.

Hayling Island

This line was famous for its use of ex-LBSCR AIX class 'Terrier' 0-6-0 tanks which worked it until closure to all traffic on 4 November 1963. The AIX class had to work the line because of the weak wooden bridge at Langstone. In the summer, the 4½-mile Havant to Hayling Island branch had a service of four trains per hour. Surviving AIXs are on the KESR, Bluebell and Isle of Wight railways including the oldest examples which date from 1872. Hayling Island to North Hayling is now a footpath, the building at Hayling having been demolished.

Havant, with an AIX 0-6-0T, No. 32650, setting off for Hayling Island with a two-coach train on 5 October 1963, a month before the closure of the line to all traffic. The engine was built at Brighton in 1876 as No. 50 *Whitechapel* and has survived into preservation on the Kent & East Sussex Railway.

A1 0-6-0T No. 78 *Knowle* is seen pulling away from Langston in 1890 with a train of four and six wheelers bound for Hayling Island. The engine was built at Brighton in June 1880, reboilered to AIX in 1911 and withdrawn by BR in 1963 having worked on the Isle of Wight and the KESR. The engine spent some time at Butlins Minehead holiday camp but has now returned to the KESR.

R. S. Carpenter

AIX No. 32650 leaves Hayling Island on 7 April 1958 with two LSWR coaches. The engine was rebuilt to AIX in 1920 and withdrawn by BR in 1963.

Another view of AIX 'Terrier' No. 32650 as it crosses the wooden bridge at Langstone with the 1.35pm Havant to Hayling Island on 26 October 1963 shortly before the line closed to all traffic.

S. C. Nash

The all-timber structure at North Hayling with No. 32650 arriving for Hayling. Opened on 17 July 1867 the branch closed to all traffic on 4 November 1963. The halt was subsequently demolished.

Hayling Island station on 7 April 1958 with No. 32650 yet again, and LSWR coaching stock. The station was opened on 17 July 1867 as South Hayling and renamed Hayling Island on 1 June 1892. The station has been demolished but 'Terier' No. 32646, formerly No. 46 *Newington* of 1876 was displayed outside the Hayling Billy public house for 13 years before going to the Isle of Wight Steam Railway.

Coaling an AIX by hand at Hayling Island in October 1963 appears to be an easy job as the bunker had been cut down when the locomotive (No. 32650) was used on the Isle of Wight.

Hythe on 8 March 1958 with Eastleigh M7 class 0-4-4T No. 30033 being watered en route to Fawley. The line is still in use for oil trains serving Fawley refinery. The station building still exists but is very dilapidated.

Fawley was opened to passengers on 20 July 1925 by the Southern Railway but the passenger service was sparse. M7 class 0-4-4T No. 30033, built at Nine Elms in 1898, has arrived at the single-platform station with a train of Maunsell stock. The passenger service was withdrawn on 14 February 1966 but the line is still well used today by oil trains. The station platform remains but is now inside the Esso premises and out of public reach.

Q class No. 30541 works the 1.28pm Lymington Pier to Waterloo on 5 September 1959 near Ampress Halt. On summer Saturdays trains from Lymington Pier were worked through to Waterloo with an engine change. The line was electrified in July 1967 with the main line modernisation scheme. This 0-6-0 has been preserved by the Maunsell Locomotive Society and can be seen today on the Bluebell Railway.

S. C. Nash

Lymington Pier with Adams T1 class 0-4-4T No. E70 running round the train from Brockenhurst in 1928. The headshunt has since been abolished and the line shortened. The hazy outline of the Isle of Wight can be discerned beyond the spotless engine which was built at Nine Elms in 1881.

H. F. Wheeller

Lymington Pier in July 1957 with M7 class 0-4-4T No. 30028 and pre-Grouping stock. The branch opened to Lymington Town on 19 September 1860 and was extended to Lymington Pier on 1 May 1884.

H. F. Wheeller

Lymington Pier to Lymington Town was opened in 1884 by the LSWR who ran their own boats to Yarmouth on the Isle of Wight. M7 class No. 30029, built at Nine Elms in 1904, is seen arriving at the Town station with a three-coach Maunsell push-and-pull unit in July 1962. The engine survived until May 1964.

Totton, Hythe & Fawley Light Railway

This was one of the lines built by the Southern Railway after Grouping and was opened on 20 July 1925. The line was 9½ miles long and had stations at Marchwood, Hythe and Fawley. The passenger service was sparse and considered secondary to the freight traffic which was to the oil refinery at Fawley owned by Esso. Passenger services were withdrawn on 14 February 1966. The line is still very much in use today for, apart from the oil traffic, there are MoD sidings at Marchwood. The station at Marchwood is complete with semaphore signals. The building at Hythe survives but is vandalised and the station platform at Fawley still exists within the massive oil refinery complex.

Brockenhurst to Lymington Pier

The 5¼-mile branch to Lymington was opened on 12 July 1858 to Lymington Town, and on 1 May 1884 to Lymington Pier. The line is still thriving, following electrification in July 1967, the present multiple units having replaced the BR Standard tanks and Maunsell stock.

Blackwater on the Sandown to Newport line as seen in the summer of 1958, two years after closure of the line to all traffic on 6 February 1956. The station house survives today but has been altered in size. The line was opened on 1 February 1875 as part of the Isle of Wight Central Railway system.

Isle of Wight Lines

The Isle of Wight system was a great attraction in steam days as all the locomotives and rolling stock dated from pre-Grouping companies. Under the Southern, the locomotives were LSWR and LBSCR, O2, E1 and AIX class tanks, whilst the rolling stock was of SECR and LBSCR origin. This situation arose as a result of the rolling stock from suburban steam lines, electrified during the 1920s, being transferred to the Isle of Wight. Some of the pre-1923 rolling stock has survived, as has an O2 class 0-4-4 tank, No. 24 *Calbourne*, and two AIX class 0-6-0Ts, now kept by the Isle of Wight Steam Railway at Haven Street.

The Isle of Wight system was grouped into the Southern Railway in 1923. The island had three constituent companies: the Isle of Wight Railway, from Ryde to Ventnor including the Bembridge branch; the Isle of Wight Central, from Ryde to Cowes, with the Ventnor West and Newport to Sandown branches; and the Freshwater, Yarmouth & Newport Railway. In addition to these three concerns, the section of main line from Ryde Pier Head to St Johns Road was jointly owned by the LSWR and the LBSCR. All of the island was steam-worked until 31 December 1966 when the remaining part of

the system from Ryde Pier Head to Shanklin was electrified with secondhand London Transport stock.

The first closures on the Island were the Ventnor West line on 15 September 1952, the Bembridge and Freshwater lines on 21 September 1953, and the Newport to Sandown line on 6 February 1956, all to all traffic. The next closures were the Ryde (Smallbrook Junction) to Cowes section on 21 February 1966 to passengers, and the Ventnor to Shanklin line on 18 April 1966 to all traffic. Freight traffic held on from Medina Wharf to Cowes until 16 May 1966, and Medina to Smallbrook Junction until 24 October 1966.

The first railway on the island was the Cowes & Newport Railway which was opened on 16 June 1862. There was no doubt that the island's railways had a character of their own. The Southern painted the engines green, named all of them and kept them spotlessly clean. The engines had Caledonian style hooters and the trains were air-braked. The countryside was unspoilt and the branch lines little used in the winter.

Today's Isle of Wight Steam Railway runs from Smallbrook Junction, constructed by Network SouthEast in

The Isle of Wight railways imported LBSCR 'Terriers' from the mainland which were in use on the Island from 1899 until 1949. No. 40 *Brighton*, built in 1878 and exhibited at the Paris Exhibition that year, was sold to the Isle of Wight Central Railway in 1902 and lasted under BR until 1963. The engine was sold to Butlins in 1964 and returned to the Island in 1973 where it was restored by the Isle of Wight Steam Railway as No. 11 in lined black livery. It returned to traffic in 1989 but is seen here at Battersea as an A1 in LBSCR days.

R. S. Carpenter

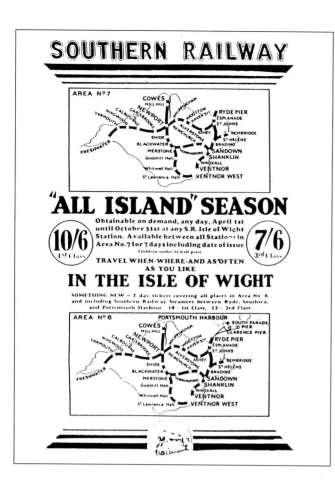

SOUTHERN RAILWAY

AREA N° 7

"ALL ISLAND" SEASON

Obtainable on demand, any day, April 1st until October 31st at any S.R. Isle of Wight Station. Available between all Stations in Area No. 7 for 7 days including date of issue
Children under 14 half price

10/6 1st Class

7/6 3rd Class

TRAVEL WHEN·WHERE·AND AS OFTEN AS YOU LIKE

IN THE ISLE OF WIGHT

SOMETHING NEW – 7 day tickets covering all places in Area No. 6 and including Southern Railway Steamers between Ryde, Southsea, and Portsmouth Harbour. 18/- 1st Class, 15/- 3rd Class.

AREA N° 6

Isle of Wight Railway.

TO

Newport

Via Sandown Junction.

Alverstone was the name of O2 class No. 29 which originated as No. 202 of the LSWR having been built at Nine Elms in August 1891. Following the 1923 Grouping the Southern Railway sent O2 class 0-4-4Ts to the Isle of Wight to replace the ageing island engines. No. 202 was shipped to the Isle of Wight in 1926 being one of 21 O2s transferred to the island between 1923 and 1949. All were subsequently named.

Hugh Ballantyne

The scene that greeted visitors to the Isle of Wight until December 1966 was one of an all steam railway. Two O2 class 0-4-4Ts wait at Ryde Pier Head as passengers disembark from their paddle steamer from Portsmouth. No. 32 *Bonchurch* on the right, and No.16 *Ventnor* on the left, were both LSWR engines of 1892 having been built at Nine Elms. The Ryde Pier tramway tracks can be seen in the foreground in this August 1958 photograph.

High Tide on Ryde Pier with O2 class No. 24 *Calbourne*, now the sole survivor, heading for Cowes on 16 September 1965. The engine was originally LSWR No. 209 built at Nine Elms in 1891 and shipped to the Island in 1925.

The last day of steam working on the Isle of Wight, 31 December 1966, sees a wreathed O2 No. 17 *Seaview* at Ryde Esplanade. No. 17, ex LSWR No. 208 built in 1891, was shipped over to the island in 1930 by the Southern.

Hugh Ballantyne

Ryde St Johns Road with O2 class 0-4-4T No. 14 *Fishbourne* with a Cowes train in the last days of steam working. The engine was built at Nine Elms in 1889 as No. 178 and transferred to the island system in 1936.

Hugh Ballantyne

Ryde St Johns with O2 class 0-4-4T No. 17 *Seaview* on 12 July 1966. The train is bound for Shanklin with a mixture of LBSCR and SECR stock. Ryde Works can be seen in the background behind the 'Brighton' stock which is berthed in the bay platform. The engine has had its original nameplate replaced.

M. Squire

O2 class No. 18 *Ningwood* scoots up the bank from Ryde St Johns with a Shanklin bound train in 1958 on duty No. 7. No.18 was built at Nine Elms by the LSWR in 1892 as No. 220 and shipped to the Isle of Wight by the SR in 1930.

Ashey was an idyllic place in the summer where the station site could become very overgrown. No. 33 *Bembridge* of 1892 pauses momentarily with a Cowes bound train. The line closed to all traffic in 1966 but has since reopened as far as Wootton. The scene today has not changed very much but the house has been fenced off as it is a private residence.

Crossing trains at Haven Street on 9 August 1959 with No. 27 *Merstone* waiting with a Ryde bound train. No. 27, built at Nine Elms in 1890 as LSWR No. 184, was taken across the Solent to the island in 1926. Haven Street was rebuilt by the Southern in 1926 who built the island platform. The location is now the headquarters of the Isle of Wight Steam Railway.

No. 29 *Alverstone* crossing No. 17 *Seaview* at Newport with a Cowes bound train in the last days of steam on the Isle of Wight. The railways to Newport closed to passenger traffic on 21 February 1966.

Hugh Ballantyne

Newport, with O2 class No. 24 passing over the River Medina on 19 February 1966. The viaduct has now been replaced by a road bridge. The engine was built at Nine Elms in 1891 by the LSWR, shipped to the Isle of Wight in 1925 and named *Calbourne*.

S. C. Nash

Newport was the centre of the island's activities with lines going off in four directions. No.24 *Calbourne*, the surviving O2 class 0-4-4T, is seen running bunker first for Ryde in September 1965. The carriage shed and engine shed were to the right of the picture but all have now been demolished and no trace of the buildings or station remain as the area has been altered by road improvements.

Taking water at Newport, O2 class No. 24 with a Cowes bound train on 26 September 1965. The engine has been restored to Southern green by the Isle of Wight Steam Railway with its coal bunker cut down to its original height. Note the coal stove by the water column to keep it from freezing in winter.

A general view of the four-platformed terminus at Cowes, opened in 1862 and modernised by the Southern Railway after 1923. No.24 *Calbourne* waits to return to Newport on 16 September 1965 in what was, at the time, a complete pre-Grouping scene with LBSCR and SECR coaches.

Yarmouth on the former Freshwater, Yarmouth & Newport Railway just before closure which took place on 21 September 1953. The line closed to all traffic but the station is still in situ, the building being used as a local community centre. The old trackbed is now a public footpath and the walk is well worth a visit as it goes round the estuary of the River Yar.

A. Burgess

No. 24 again, but now nameless, is seen at Mill Hill on 26 September 1965 with a Cowes bound train. The station building has been demolished and the site built over.

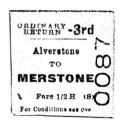

Cowes with No. 29 *Alverstone* propelling the stock out of the platform. The railway was opened as the Cowes & Newport Railway on 16 June 1862 and later became part of the Isle of Wight Central Railway. The station has been demolished and little remains to be seen today.

Hugh Ballantyne

Freshwater, at the end of the line from Newport, was closed from 21 September 1953. The station site is now occupied by a supermarket. The O2 class 0-4-4T, No.33 *Bembridge* of 1892, was shipped over to the island in 1936.

Lens of Sutton

Ventnor West on the occasion of the last day with No. 27 *Merstone* posed at the end of the platform, 13 September 1952. No. 27 was originally LSWR No. 184 of 1890 and was shipped to the Isle of Wight in 1926. The engine has certainly been spruced up in this shot with the BR post 1948 livery looking quite smart.

Pamlin Prints

The former IWCR station building at Ventnor, renamed Ventnor West by the Southern after 1923, has been incorporated into a housing development. The Ventnor West line was closed to all traffic by BR on 15 September 1952 having been opened in 1897 as the Newport, Godshill & St Lawrence Railway.

Lens of Sutton

Last day at Shanklin with Nos 24 and 31 on 31 December 1966. The train was organised by the LCGB – double- headers being a rare commodity on the island.

Hugh Ballantyne

Shanklin is now the terminus of the line from Ryde Pier Head where ex London Transport tube stock now handle the traffic. No. 26 *Whitwell* departs from the station with a Ventnor train in August 1958.

Wroxall on 9 April 1966 with No. 31 *Chale* heading for Ventnor with the 1.25pm Ryde Pier Head to Ventnor. The station was well known for the Station Hotel which was adjacent to the up platform.

Smallbrook Junction in the final days of steam with an O2 class 0-4-4T arriving from Ventnor. The railway was double track from this point to Ryde, but during the winter both lines worked as single tracks. The site is now occupied by Smallbrook Junction station, opened in 1989 as an interchange between the steam railway and the electrified line to Shanklin.

Pamlin Prints

Ventnor was the end of the line and No. 33 *Bembridge,* ex LSWR No. 218 of 1891, takes water after arrival from Ryde. The line from Shanklin was closed by BR on 18 April 1966 to all traffic. The station was unusual in that a wooden bridge was placed over the tracks to enable passengers to get to the centre platform.

Hugh Ballantyne

1991, to the Isle of Wight Steam Railway terminus at Wooton, a short distance from the former BR station which was situated on the other side of the road in a cutting. The present steam railway gives a good impression of what travel was like on the island before steam finished in December 1966. Isle of Wight Steam Railway trains connect at Smallbrook with the electric trains for Ryde which run from Shanklin. Relics of the rest of the system can be seen today as some of the closed stations have been turned into private residences.

On the former Freshwater, Yarmouth & Newport Railway, the station site at Freshwater is now occupied by a supermarket whilst Yarmouth station is now a community centre. Ningwood is a house, whilst Calbourne has a new house built over the former station. At Watchingwell the former private station still exists, but Carisbrooke has been built over. On the Newport to Cowes section a lot of the line has been built over, and the site at Newport has disappeared under road improvements. Whippingham station is now a well preserved private house like Ashey which has been fenced off from the present railway. Bembridge station site is now a housing estate, but St Helens is now a house. On the former Ventnor West line, the station building at Ventnor West survives in a housing development as do the other three stations which are now private residences. Ventnor and Wroxall stations have been demolished but the old caves at Ventnor are still in use by contractors. On the Sandown to Newport branch (closed in 1956) Alvestone and Horringford stations survive as houses while Blackwater station house exists in an enlarged form. Merstone and Newchurch have been demolished and Shide has been built over.

Scenes on the former Freshwater branch at Carisbrooke, the first station out from Newport, in 1953. The former Freshwater, Yarmouth & Newport Railway was closed to all traffic on 21 September 1953. The upper scene shows the station from rail level and the lower view depicts the Southern concrete standard nameboard still with wartime white stripes.

J. H. Aston and Lens of Sutton

Branch Lines in Wiltshire, Somerset and Dorset

Bulford Camp

The LSWR opened the 8-mile long branch to Amesbury on 1 October 1901, and to Bulford on 1 June 1906. The line was built primarily for the military traffic on Salisbury Plain. There was a direct connection off the branch facing Salisbury to Porton which was opened on 8 August 1904. The branch had ten trains per day in June 1914, but by 1952 this had been reduced to one train per day. The line closed to passengers on 30 June 1952 and to freight on 4 March 1963, the last train being a railtour organised by the Railway Enthusiasts Club of Farnborough on 23 March 1963. The train was a push-and-pull unit hauled by M7 class 0-4-4T No. 30108. The direct connection from Amesbury Junction to Newton Tony Junction closed to all traffic on 30 June 1952, the same day that the passenger service was withdrawn. The stations have been built over or demolished.

Salisbury (Alderbury Junction) to West Moors

The 23½-mile Salisbury to West Moors line opened on 20 December 1866 and was independent until purchased by the LSWR in 1883. The line was secondary to the more direct route but was useful as a diversionary line to Bournemouth. There was always a through train from Waterloo to Weymouth by this route, which was detached from the overnight newspaper train at Salisbury. This line also had its fair share of long-distance holiday trains on summer Saturdays in the post-war period. Passenger traffic to seaside resorts grew to enormous sizes during the period 1945 to 1960, the peak being reached in 1958. Bournemouth and Poole were favourite places for visitors and trains would come from all over the country on Saturdays in the summer.

The line closed to all traffic on 4 May 1964. All five intermediate stations were excellent examples of LSWR architecture and were in Southern Railway colours at closure. LSWR signalling also survived until closure and so did some of the LSWR enamel nameboards on the stations. West Moors to Wimborne is now a road – the 5½-mile Ferndown bypass. Downton station has been built over but Breamore survives having been purchased by Hampshire County Council. Fordingbridge has been obliterated by an industrial

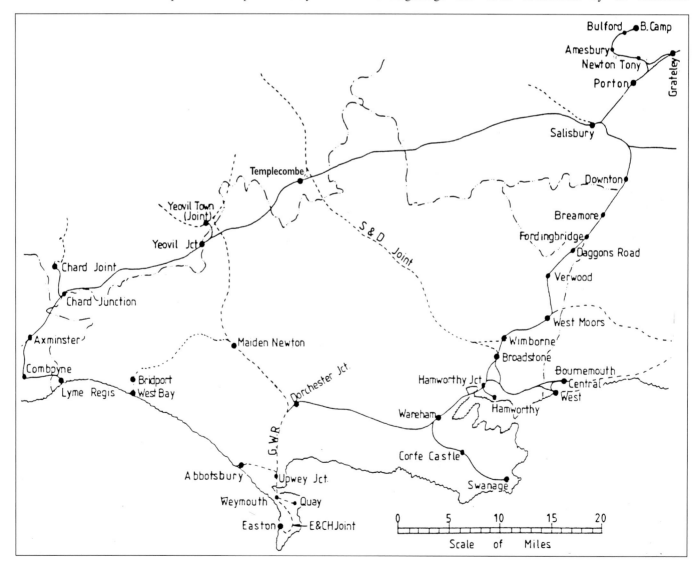

Amesbury was one of the intermediate stations on the former LSWR Bulford branch, opened on 29 April 1902, to serve military camps in the area. The Railway Enthusiasts Club organised a special, the 'Rambling Rose', to Bulford on 23 March 1963 with M7 class No. 30108 of 1904 and a Maunsell push-and-pull set. The site has now been occupied by an industrial estate.

Bulford had a sparse service out of the war years and passenger trains were withdrawn by BR in 1952. The line remained open for freight until 4 March 1963. Here, T9 class 4-4-0 No. 30719 is seen about to depart with a van train to Amesbury on 2 June 1952.

S. C. Nash

Amesbury, with Beattie well tank No. 30587 on 14 May 1955 heading an REC special. The line was extended to Bulford by the LSWR on 1 June 1906 to serve military camps. The Beattie 2-4-0 well tanks usually worked out from Wadebridge but No. 30587 was brought up for the special and is seen here with LSWR stock. Two of the class, built in 1874, have survived and today, No. 30587 can be seen at the Buckinghamshire Railway Centre, Quainton Road.

R. S. Carpenter

Standard Class 4 4-6-0 No. 75067 stops at Downton with the 8.22pm Salisbury to Bournemouth Central on 4 June 1960. The prominent feature here is the LSWR black and white enamel nameboard but the mat in the signal box still had 'LSWR' upon it, underneath the photographer's feet! The line closed to all traffic on 4 May 1964 and the site is now covered by houses.

Hugh Ballantyne

Breamore (Hants) station, seen here in the summer of 1962, just two years before closure, appears to be a tranquil spot. The LSWR thoughtfully planted trees behind the station house to enhance the location which quite remarkably enough remains little changed today as the local council have purchased the site for a road bypass which is yet to be built. The track has been removed but all the buildings are intact.

Fordingbridge still retains the original LSWR nameboards in this July 1962 view of the station which is complete with goods yard at the rear. The station, little changed since pre-Grouping days in this photograph, has now been demolished and the site turned into an industrial estate.

N class 2-6-0 No. 31622, built at Ashford in January 1929, survived until January 1964. The engine was going to be built as a K class 2-6-4 tank by the Southern Railway but they changed their plans after the 1927 Sevenoaks accident. The Mogul is seen here passing Fordingbridge with the 9am Bournemouth Central to Cardiff on 18 July 1953.

S. C. Nash

Daggons Road on the Salisbury to West Moors line is seen here in faded SR colours shortly before closure. The LSWR oil lamps are still in their war time paint with white stripes. The passing loop did not have a platform and was controlled by the neat little ground frame with a pagoda roof, left. The houses survive in a new building development which has covered the site.

Crossing trains at Wimborne with BR Standard Class 4 2-6-0 No. 76028 heading for Salisbury with a train from Bournemouth. The service to Salisbury was withdrawn on 4 May 1964 and the station at Wimborne demolished, the site now being occupied by a road.

development, Daggons Road is now a new housing estate and Verwood has been demolished, but the station pub, The Albion, survives. West Moors station has been built over and is now a new housing estate.

Hamworthy and Bournemouth West
The 1½-mile Hamworthy branch opened on 1 June 1847, the station being known as Poole. The line closed to passengers on 1 July 1896, but today is still open to freight. The line has

at times been visited by various railtours over the years.

Bournemouth West terminus opened on 15 June 1874 became part of the LSWR system and was the terminus for Somerset & Dorset Railway trains. Summer Saturday trains in the years prior to the S&D closure came from Derby, Bradford, Sheffield, Manchester, Bristol, Birmingham and Nottingham. Bournemouth West station closed to passengers on 4 October 1965 and the station site has now been redeveloped in connection with a new road scheme.

Swanage terminus with M7 class 0-4-4T No. 30129 of 1906 sizzling quietly with a two-coach Maunsell set in May 1963. The line, which was opened by the LSWR in 1885, was closed by BR on 3 January 1972. The station is now the terminus and headquarters of the Swanage Railway.

Corfe Castle Viaduct was a well-known location on the Swanage branch, where Q class 0-6-0 No. 30541 is seen working an up freight on 17 June 1957.

S. C. Nash

Corfe Castle, a famous tourist spot, was one of those buildings which was 'knocked about a bit' during the Civil War. It has always been a problem to photograph as it is on the wrong side of the line for the light. M7 class No. 30052 races past the old ruin with a two-coach Maunsell set on 18 May 1963.

Bulleid Pacifics worked through to Swanage and No. 34042 *Dorchester*, a Bournemouth engine, is seen near Furzebrook on 23 August 1958 with the 1.23pm Saturdays only ex Waterloo. The train consists of a hotch potch of Maunsell, Bulleid and BR standard coaches in SR green or BR red and cream.

S. C. Nash

Swanage

The Swanage branch was opened on 20 May 1885 by the LSWR and was 11 miles long. The line closed completely on 2 January 1972, the section from Worgret Junction to Furzebrook being retained for oil trains serving a newly discovered oil producing area of Britain. At the other end of the former branch is the Swanage Railway Company, another fast-growing steam railway, which runs trains for the public from Swanage to Norden near Corfe Castle and is being extended to connect up with the national network at Furzebrook.

Portland and Easton

The branch to Portland was opened on 16 October 1865, and was owned jointly by the LSWR and the GWR, becoming BR Southern Region at nationalisation in 1948. The line was extended to Easton, a distance of 8½-miles, on 1 September 1902. Easton to Melcombe Regis (Weymouth) closed on 3 March 1952 to passengers, and freight from 5 April 1965.

Yeovil Junction to Yeovil Town

Yeovil Junction to Yeovil Town (1¾ miles) was opened by the LSWR on 1 June 1861, the station at Yeovil Town being jointly owned with the GWR. In Southern days the line was worked by an M7 class 0-4-4T and a push-and-pull unit – the train being known locally as the 'Bunk'. The passenger service was withdrawn on 3 October 1966 and the site of the town station has since become a car park.

Chard Junction to Chard Town

The 3¼-mile line from Chard Junction to Chard was opened on 8 May 1863. The LSWR had a station at Chard Town but when the Bristol & Exeter Railway arrived on the scene on 11 September 1866 a new joint station was opened, with broad gauge from Taunton on one platform and standard gauge from Chard Junction on the other. The LSWR terminus at Chard Town was closed on 30 December 1916 and the line worked entirely by the GWR to Chard Junction. The Chard Joint station was renamed Chard Central by BR in 1949, and the GWR branch became part of the Southern Region from 2 April 1950. This was later returned to the Western Region in 1958. Chard Junction to Chard Central closed to all traffic on 30 October 1966, the GWR branch from Taunton (Creech Junction) having closed to all traffic on 6 July 1964. The passenger service from Chard Junction to Town was withdrawn on 10 September 1962. A feature of the Chard Central station layout was the long interchange platform for transhipment of goods between the standard and broad gauges. This platform could be seen until closure in 1966. The building survives as a road vehicle testing station.

A short branch connected Yeovil Junction with Yeovil Town and M7 class No. 30129 can be seen here propelling up the hill towards the Junction station. The line was closed by BR on 3 October 1966 and the Town station site converted to a car park.

Chard Junction was a Southern station with a separate platform for Chard Central trains. These were worked by the GWR under an agreement between the two companies after the LSWR closed its own terminus at Chard Town on 30 December 1916. BR operated the line until 30 October 1966 and 0-6-0 pannier tank No. 3736 can be seen in this July 1962 view with ex GWR stock.

Lyme Regis station was in Dorset but the line originated from Axminster in Devon, 6¾ miles away. Adams radial tank No. 30582 can be seen in the platform during the winter when only one coach was needed to cater for passengers. The Maunsell composite brake is about to be loaded with parcels and, in the lower view, the single-road engine shed can be seen through the mist. Photographs taken on 1 January 1961.

The most noticeable engineering feature on the Lyme Regis branch was the crooked viaduct at Cannington where Adams 4-4-2T No. 30583 is seen with a single-coach train. The viaduct is still in position and can be seen today.

Adams 4-4-2T No. 30584, built in 1885 by Dübs, pauses for a short while at Combpyne on the Lyme Regis branch on 13 September 1956. The coach was a LSWR tri composite brake but only used for two classes under the SR.

Combpyne Halt was a remote spot on the Lyme Regis branch and Adams radial tank No. 30582 can be seen here with a train of Maunsell coaches. Water is being unloaded for the railway cottages and camping coach in this July 1960 view.

Andrew C. Ingram collection

Double heading on the Lyme Regis branch took place on Saturdays during the summer when through coaches were worked from Waterloo. Nos 30582 and 30583, both Adams 4-4-2 tanks, are seen here at Trill with the 10.45am from Waterloo on 10 September 1960.

S. C. Nash

Engines Nos 30583 and 30584 are seen working the 4.36pm Axminster to Lyme Regis in May 1960 near Combpyne. The line was opened as the Axminster & Lyme Regis Railway on 24 August 1903 and closed by BR on 29 November 1965. No 30583 of 1885 has been preserved and can be seen today on the Bluebell Railway.

S. C. Nash

Axminster to Lyme Regis

The Axminster & Lyme Regis Light Railway was 6¾ miles long and opened on 24 August 1903. There was only one intermediate station at Compyne, near Cannington Viaduct, the principal engineering feature on the line. The viaduct had to be reinforced shortly after opening in 1903 as the land subsided and a support had to be put in the third arch. The concrete viaduct can still be seen today. The LSWR used AIX class 0-6-0Ts to start with, then O2 class 0-4-4Ts but these were superseded by the well-known Adams 4-4-2 tanks which worked the line until 1960 when they were replaced by Ivatt 2-6-2Ts. One of the Adams engines, No. 488 (BR No. 30583)

survives on the Bluebell Railway, Sussex. This locomotive also worked on the ill-fated East Kent Railway. The line eventually became dieselised but closed to all traffic on 29 November 1965. A feature of train operation was that on summer Saturdays during the post-war period, through trains were run to Lyme Regis from Waterloo. For this operation the trains were double-headed by the Adams tanks. The severe curvature of the track guaranteed the survival of these locomotives until track improvements were carried out in 1960 enabling the Ivatt Class 2s to be used. Lyme Regis station site is now an industrial estate but Compyne station house survives and is named The Sidings.

Branch Lines in Devon and Cornwall

Seaton Junction to Seaton

The Seaton branch of 4½ miles was opened on 16 March 1868 as the Seaton & Beer Railway, which was later bought by the LSWR. There were two stations on the line, at Colyton and Colyford. The line in post-war years was worked by LSWR M7 tanks and railmotor sets until their displacement by GWR panniers and 1400 class 0-4-2Ts after the line became part of the Western Region from 1 January 1963. The branch closed to all traffic on 7 March 1966 but that was not the end of the Seaton branch. In September 1969, the miniature tramway at Eastbourne closed, was packed up and relaid on the trackbed of the BR Seaton branch. The 2ft 9in gauge Seaton Tramway, as it is known, was opened on 28 August 1970 to Colyford. The electric tramway was extended to Colyton in 1977, and operates a well-patronised tourist service, the tramcars being approximately ⅔ scale of a standard gauge version. The reopened line is 3 miles long and terminates at the old LSWR station at Colyton. The section from here to what was Seaton Junction has been lifted. Seaton station site is now occupied by an industrial concern, the tramway having an attractive, specially built terminus.

Railways to Exmouth and Sidmouth

The line from Sidmouth Junction to Sidmouth opened on 6 July 1874 as the Sidmouth Railway. The connecting line from Tipton St Johns to Exmouth via Budleigh Salterton opened throughout on 1 June 1903. The Sidmouth Railway was worked by the LSWR but remained independent until 1922. The 3¼-mile Sidmouth branch closed to passengers on 6 March 1967, the same day as the Exmouth to Tipton St Johns section. Freight trains ceased to run to Sidmouth on 8 May 1967 from Sidmouth Junction. Sidmouth Junction station reopened on 3 May 1971 as Feniton served by Exeter-London, Waterloo trains. The section from Tipton St Johns to Exmouth also closed to all traffic on 6 March 1967. Today, only the direct line to Exmouth from Exeter (Exmouth Junction), opened on 6 March 1861, is still in use. An unusual working, prior to the closure of the Somerset & Dorset line in 1966, was the through train from Exmouth and Sidmouth to Cleethorpes. This train ran on summer Saturdays only and joined up at Tipton prior to reversal on to the main line at Sidmouth Junction. Trains were run between holiday resorts, as many people had a week in each resort. Ottery St Mary

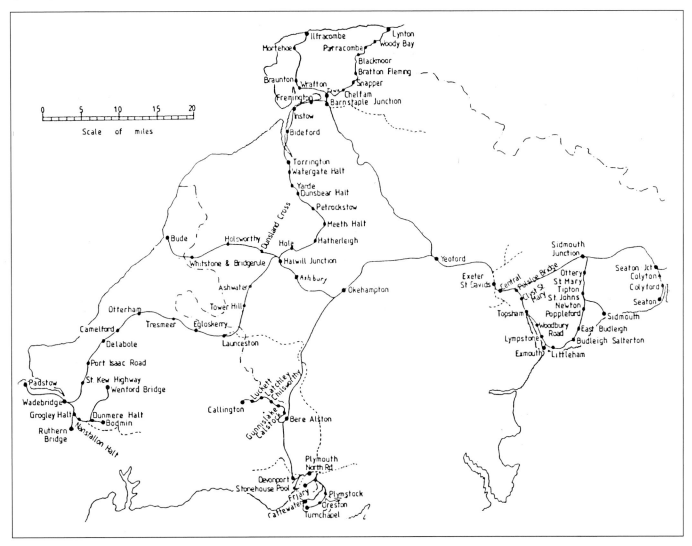

Seaton during the Western Region era in 1965 when ex GWR types appeared on the branch. A 6400 class pannier and single coach with fold down steps waits for passengers during the final years of the line which closed to all traffic on 7 March 1966.

Hugh Ballantyne

Seaton before the Western Region takeover with Southern engines and stock. The M7 0-4-4T, No. 30125, is seen 'on shed' having been detached from the Maunsell two-coach set which is resting in the platform. The station was very much rebuilt by the SR in pre-war years having been opened originally by the Seaton & Beer Railway on 16 March 1868.

Seaton station on 12 July 1962 with M7 class 0-4-4T No. 30125 of 1911 and train loading up for the 4½-mile run to Seaton Junction.

Colyford in April 1957 with M7 class 0-4-4T No. 30480 and eager passengers awaiting the train's arrival. The line was closed by BR in 1966 but this part of the trackbed is now occupied by the Seaton Tramway, a 2ft 9in gauge concern that opened on 28 August 1970. The engine survived until May 1964.

The Western Region took over lines west of Salisbury on 1 January 1963 and, as a result, some of the old LSWR lines were 'Westernised'. GWR 0-4-2T No. 1450 appeared on the Seaton branch, complete with a single auto coach which can be seen here at Colyford on 2 February 1965. No. 1450 has survived and is one of the four members of the class in existence.

M7 class No. 30125 potters out of Colyton bound for Seaton Junction on 12 July 1962. The scene has altered and the tracks are now those of the narrow gauge tramway which terminates here. The overhead wire electric tramway was opened through to Colyton in 1977 with the old LSWR building being retained as the passenger terminus.

Colyton of the former LSWR with a Great Western train hauled by 1400 class 0-4-2T No. 1450 on 2 February 1965.

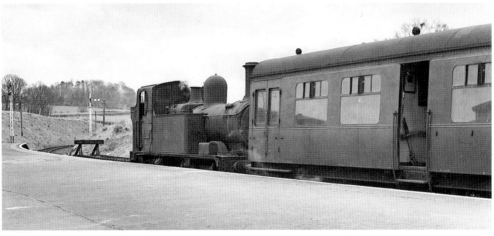

A fine study of a GWR auto train seen here in the Seaton bay platform at Seaton Junction. The interior of the unit with the lever for lowering the steps can be discerned. The smaller compartment is the non smoker in this 1965 view.

M7 class No. 30025 leaves Sidmouth on 23 August 1954 with a train of LSWR stock bound for Sidmouth Junction which is now known as Feniton. Opened as the Sidmouth Railway on 6 July 1874 the single-tracked line was closed to all traffic by BR on 8 May 1967. The station site at Sidmouth is now an industrial estate but the old station buildings survive.

H. F. Wheeller

Sidmouth Junction with M7 class No. 30025 leaving for Sidmouth on 28 August 1954. The main line can be seen in the background with the LSWR signal box and semaphores. The Sidmouth branch closed to passengers on 6 March 1967, the same day as the Exmouth line. Sidmouth Junction reopened as Feniton on 3 May 1971.

H. F. Wheeller

Early BR days at Tipton St Johns with M7 class No. 256 and LSWR stock. The LSWR nameboard in black and white enamel has survived into the Nationalisation period. This was the junction for the Sidmouth branch and the line to Exmouth.

Lens of Sutton

Tipton St Johns in August 1954 with new Class 3 2-6-2T No. 82019 running in with an Exmouth train. The Standard Class 3 tanks were designed at Swindon and introduced in 1952, Exmouth Junction receiving an allocation of ten of the class. The station site is now a small park.

H. F. Wheeller

Budleigh Salterton on 26 August 1954 with Class 3 2-6-2T No. 82018 on an Exmouth to Sidmouth Junction train which includes a through coach to Waterloo. The line was opened by the LSWR on 1 June 1903. The site is now occupied by a supermarket.

H. F. Wheeller

Littleham on the Exmouth to Sidmouth Junction line in April 1957 with an O2 class 0-4-4T crossing a Class 3 2-6-2T on an Exmouth train. The line was closed to all traffic on 6 March 1967. Exmouth Junction shed had an allocation of three O2s at the time, No. 30193 of 1890 being one of them.

Topsham on 19 April 1957 on the direct line from Exeter to Exmouth with some LSWR characteristics and a row of LSWR barrows. The ornate valancing was a feature of some LSWR stations. The substantial station buildings probably dated from the line's opening on 1 May 1861.

Class 3 2-6-2T No. 82010 crosses the River Test on 10 April 1957 with a train of BR standard compartment stock near Topsham. The Class 3 2-6-2Ts were brought in to replace the ageing M7 class 0-4-4Ts on the Exeter to Exmouth line. No members of the class have survived into preservation.

Lympstone on the Exmouth line with Class 3 2-6-2T No. 82019 running in with an Exmouth bound train. LSWR signals with lower quadrant arms are a feature here, as is the LSWR loop shunt signal by the locomotive.

Barnstaple Junction, once the junction for the Ilfracombe, Torrington and Taunton lines, is now the terminus of the single-track line from Exeter. Ivatt Class 2 2-6-2T No. 41283 is seen in May 1964 with a train of ex GWR stock bound for Torrington.

station has survived in an industrial estate, Tipton St Johns and East Budleigh are houses but the rest of the stations have been demolished or built over except Sidmouth station buildings which survive as offices with the rest of the site in use as an industrial estate.

Barnstaple to Ilfracombe
The 15 miles from Barnstaple Junction to Ilfracombe could be classified as a branch line, or the end of the main line from Waterloo. Ilfracombe, 226 miles 16 chains from Waterloo, had a through service. The through services from Waterloo to Devon and Cornwall were legendary and the trains could consist of nine portions, one for each destination. Ilfracombe could end up with one coach from Barnstaple Junction in the winter, the load being an easy one for a 'West Country' class Pacific. The line opened on 20 July 1874 and included some stiff gradients – 1 in 40 up to Mortehoe, and 1 in 36 down into Ilfracombe over a 2¼-mile length which necessitated freight trains being banked. The Ilfracombe line even had an all-Pullman service which commenced on 20 June 1947. The train, the 'Devon Belle', left Waterloo at 12 noon, ran non-stop to Wilton where there was an engine change, and split at Exeter, one part going to Ilfracombe and the other part going

to Plymouth. The train lasted until 1954, a feature being the observation cars, one of which can now be seen on the Torbay Steam Railway. The line closed on 5 October 1970 to regular passenger trains but was not lifted until 1975, the last train being an engineers' saloon on 26 February 1975. There was a proposal to preserve the railway, the North Devon Railway Society being inaugurated in 1971. A company was floated but nothing came of it, so BR sold off the parts of the line that it could. Braunton to Barnstaple is now a public footpath, and so is Ilfracombe to Mortehoe. Barnstaple Town station is now an Indian restaurant, Wrafton a house, Braunton a health care centre, and Morthoe a theme park which opened in 1987.

Lynton & Barnstaple Railway
Much has been written about the Southern's 19½-mile 2ft gauge railway and the way in which it was closed down on 30 September 1935 and lifted shortly afterwards. Regrettably the line, which nowadays would have considerable tourist potential, was treated by its owner purely on economic grounds. The Southern Railway were very cost-conscious and if they had a bad case they simply hacked a branch off. The railway opened on 11 May 1898, ran through fine countryside, possessed some excellent Manning, Wardle 2-6-2 tanks and

Barnstaple Town sees Bulleid 4-6-2 No. 34054 *Lord Beaverbrook* heading for Ilfracombe on 5 May 1964. The Ilfracombe line was closed on 5 October 1970 and some of the old trackbed converted to a footpath.

Woody Bay station of the former Lynton & Barnstaple Railway has survived and is seen here on 3 May 1964 having been converted into a private house. The railway, closed in 1935 by the Southern, is slowly being revived and the station has now been purchased by the Lynton & Barnstaple Railway Association who are developing the site for future operations.

Snapper Halt in 1938 looking towards Barnstaple with an isolated L&BR coach in situ on the old 1ft 11½ gauge trackbed. The railway closed to all traffic on 30 September 1935 having been opened to the public on 16 May 1898. Two coaches, Nos 6991 and 6993, were preserved at this spot initially.

L&GRP

The odd man out of the Lynton & Barnstaple Railway's locomotive roster was the Baldwin 2-4-2 side tank, *Lyn*, seen here in ex works condition. The engine was ordered from Baldwins, in the USA and built in 1898 with builder's No. 15965 and cut up in Barnstaple after the line closed.

L&GRP

Barnstaple Town in 1933 with No. 760 *Exe* in the bay platform. The railway only had two years to go when this photograph was taken. Three Manning, Wardle 2-6-2 tanks were built for the 1898 opening and another, built in 1925, survived to be sent to Brazil but the whereabouts of this locomotive and its possible continued existence have became a mystery.

H. F. Wheeller

was missed by all those who were lucky enough to see it. There are one or two relics still to be seen, including the original terminus at Lynton (now a house), Woody Bay station and Bratton Fleming station. The viaduct at Chelfam still exists and there have been some very interesting developments recently as the Lynton & Barnstaple Railway Association has purchased some land and Woody Bay station. Trains will be running again over a short section at some stage in the future.

Barnstaple to Torrington

This line had an interesting history in that part of it was broad gauge and opened to Bideford on 2 November 1855. The LSWR appeared on the scene and laid standard gauge to Bideford which was opened on 2 March 1863, the line being dual gauge from Exeter. The broad gauge lasted until April 1877. The LSWR extended 5½ miles onwards from Bideford to Torrington on 18 July 1872 – this was known as the

Ivatt Class 2 2-6-2T No. 41283 leaves Torrington on 3 May 1964 with a train of ex GWR stock bound for Barnstaple Junction. The Torrington line was closed to regular passenger trains on 4 October 1965 but remained open for china clay trains. BR ran the last passenger train on 16 November 1982.

Ivatt Class 2 2-6-2T No. 41294 arrives at Torrington with a mixed train from Petrockstow on 29 August 1959. The train consists of china clay wagons behind a Bulleid composite brake corridor coach.

D. Trevor Rowe

Petrockstow with 2-6-2T No. 41297 on 7 November 1959 waiting time with a Torrington to Halwill train on the former North Devon & Cornwall Junction Light Railway. The line was opened by the SR on 27 July 1925 and closed by BR on 1 March 1965, the portion from Meeth to Halwill being closed to all traffic.

Ivatt Class 2 2-6-2T No. 41216 heads a light load of one Bulleid composite brake coach near Hatherleigh on 2 May 1964.

Hatherleigh station on the Southern's Torrington to Halwill line with Class 2 2-6-2T No. 41216 in the pouring rain on 2 May 1964. The line was planned by the LSWR but was opened by the Southern as late as 1925. The engineer in charge was Colonel H. F. Stephens who utilized 6½ miles of the 3ft gauge Torrington & Marland Railway.

E1/R class 0-6-2T No. 32610 is seen at Hatherleigh on 20 June 1949 on the 10.40am Halwill to Torrington with a single LSWR coach in SR colours. The third class is still indicated on the doors of the brake composite coach. The E1/R class were Maunsell rebuilds of the former LBSCR E1 class 0-6-0Ts.

S. C. Nash

Torrington Extension Railway. China clay was being excavated by the North Devon Clay Co. at Meeth and a 3ft gauge railway, the Torrington & Marland Railway, was constructed in 1880 to convey clay over the 6½ miles to Torrington where the line joined the LSWR. The Torrington & Marland Railway was opened for mineral traffic only on 1 January 1881. The narrow gauge line lasted until it was replaced by the standard gauge Torrington to Halwill line in 1925. Barnstaple to Petrockstow is now a footpath known as the Tarka Trail.

Torrington to Halwill (North Devon & Cornwall Junction Light Railway)

The extension southwards from Torrington had been planned by the LSWR but World War I and the railway Grouping delayed opening until 27 July 1925 by the Southern Railway. The engineer in charge was the redoubtable Colonel H. F. Stephens, the line being constructed to the standard gauge utilising the 6½ miles of the 3ft Torrington & Marland Railway. The line was dual gauge over the Torrington and Marland section when opened, and was 20 miles long when complete. Passenger traffic was sparse with the Southern using E1/R class locomotives – these were Stroudley E1 class 0-6-0 tanks rebuilt for use in the area with larger bunkers and a pair of trailing wheels. The E1/R class were ousted eventually by Ivatt Class 2, 2-6-2 tanks in the mid-fifties – these in turn giving way to a single unit diesel railcar in the sixties. The passenger service from Torrington to Halwill was

withdrawn on 1 March 1965. The portion of the line from Halwill to Meeth was closed to all traffic and lifted in 1966. Meeth goods was officially closed on 16 October 1982, the last run being in August 1982. Passenger services from Torrington to Barnstaple ceased on 4 October 1965, but there were specials and railtours after that, including Joanes specials for enthusiasts, day trippers and Christmas shoppers to Paddington. The last train to Torrington from Barnstaple was organised by BR and ran on 6 November 1982, originating from Bristol. The stations have been turned over to a variety of uses – Torrington is now a restaurant, Bideford is a branch of the Midland Bank, and Instow a marina office. Hole station survives but Halwill is now a housing estate. Hatherleigh is a house but Fremington has been demolished.

Halwill to Bude

The line from Okehampton to Bude was opened on 20 January 1879 as far as Holsworthy – the extension to Bude being opened by the LSWR on 10 August 1898. The 18½-mile line to Bude inclueded stations at Whitstone, Holsworthy and Dunsland Cross. The services on the line included through coaches from the multi-portioned 'Atlantic Coast Express' which left Waterloo at 11am and arrived at Bude at 4.12pm. On summer Saturdays the 'ACE', which ran in nine portions, would be split into two trains, one serving North Devon and the other serving North Cornwall.

Closure of the Bude branch took place with effect from 3 October 1966 to all traffic with the stations still very much in

Whitstone & Bridgerule on the Bude branch, 2 May 1964, remains very much unchanged since the day it was opened by the LSWR on 10 August 1898. An Ivatt 2-6-2T can be seen on a Bude train consisting of Maunsell stock. The old LSWR enamel black and white nameboard still adorns the up platform in this view, taken two years before closure.

The exterior of Bude station on 7 November 1959 shows a Southern Railway sign on the substantial buildings of the former LSWR. The line was closed to all traffic on 30 October 1966 and the station site is now a housing estate located in Bulleid Way.

The spacious layout at Bude as seen on 2 May 1964 – two years before closure. The station has an island platform and a 2-6-2T can be seen 'on shed'. Another Class 2 tank lurks in the station but goods traffic remains light as the goods shed is empty. Bude station site is now a housing estate.

their original condition. For example, Whitstone & Bridgerule still had its original LSWR black and white enamel nameboards at the time of closure. Bude station site is now a housing estate in Bulleid Way.

Halwill to Padstow

The North Cornwall Railway, as this outpost of the LSWR was known to railway staff, closed to all traffic between Wadebridge and Meldon Junction on 3 October 1966 – the same day as the Bude line closure. Padstow had through services to Waterloo by way of the 'Atlantic Coast Express', the line having been completed to Padstow on 27 March 1899. The distance between Padstow and Halwill was 49¾ miles with eleven intermediate stations. At Launceston the line had a connection with the GWR branch from Plymouth, which closed to all traffic on 28 February 1966. There is now a narrow gauge railway at Launceston, operating a tourist service. The 1ft 11½in gauge line, known as the Launceston Steam Railway is worked by Hunslet 0-4-0 saddle tanks from Penryn and Dinorwic slate quarries. Most of the stations from the original line survive as private houses. Egloskerry is open for bed and breakfast and Camelford has been converted to house the National Museum of Cycling.

Bodmin and Wadebridge

The Bodmin & Wadebridge Railway opened on 4 July 1834 and was one of the earliest railways in the West of England – the distance from Bodmin North to Wadebridge being 6¼ miles. The connecting line from Bodmin General to Boscarne Junction was built by the GWR and opened in 1887. This resulted in the curious layout at Bodmin whereby the LSWR and the GWR had their own stations in the town (Bodmin North and Bodmin General in BR days). GWR trains would

work through from Bodmin Road to Wadebridge via Bodmin General. Bodmin Road is now known as Bodmin Parkway. The Bodmin & Wadebridge was eventually absorbed into the LSWR after that company had reached Wadebridge via the North Cornwall line. Bodmin North to Dunmere Junction closed to all traffic on 30 January 1967, as did the Wadebridge to Padstow line. Wadebridge to Boscarne Junction closed to all traffic on 5 September 1978 but the last train ran on 17 December 1978 – a charter by Bodmin Lions from Bodmin Road to Wadebridge and back, ran twice. The closure of Wadebridge and Bodmin North left the Wenford Bridge china clay line isolated as a mineral branch from Bodmin Road to Wenford via Bodmin General and Boscarne Junction. The present Bodmin & Wenford Railway, now operating from Bodmin General to Parkway will shortly be reopening to Boscarne. Wadebridge station is now the Betjeman Centre in commemoration of poet John Betjeman.

Wenford Bridge and Ruthern Bridge

The branch from Wadebridge (Grogley Junction) to Ruthern Bridge was a mineral-only line and was closed by the Southern Railway on 30 December 1933, the last train running on 29 November 1933. This branch, like the neighbouring Wenford Bridge line, opened as early as 30 September 1834, as part of the original Bodmin & Wadebridge Railway. Both the Wenford and Ruthern lines were mineral lines only. The Wenford Bridge line was well known for the Beattie well tanks of LSWR fame – two of these 2-4-0s surviving as preserved museum pieces. The Wenford Bridge to Bodmin Road china clay line survived until 29 August 1985. The Padstow to Wenford section is now the Camel Trail footpath and cycle way with bikes available for hire at either end of the trail.

Halwill Junction sees T9 class No. 30719 arriving with a Padstow train in November 1959. The train consists of a Maunsell four-coach set with a PMV leading. The line was closed to all traffic on 3 October 1966, from Wadebridge to Meldon Junction.

Egloskerry sees N class 2-6-0 No. 31842 on a northbound train from Wadebridge on 2 May 1964, shortly before closure. The signalman is seen walking down the platform after having collected the staff. The station is now a residence and guest house and is available for visitors as a bed and breakfast establishment.

Otterham on the former North Cornwall line in May 1964 with N class No. 31849 and a lightweight freight. The N class 2-6-0s replaced the T9s on this remote piece of line from 1959.

Camelford with N class No. 31834 on a lightweight passenger train shortly before closure of the North Cornwall line. The line was completed through to Wadebridge on 1 June 1895 by the LSWR. Through coaches were provided by the Southern to Waterloo including a portion for the famous 'Atlantic Coast Express'.

N class No. 31812 was a pre-Grouping engine having been built at Ashford in August 1920 for the SECR. The 2-6-0 did not last much longer after this photograph was taken at Delabole as it was withdrawn from service in June 1964, one month later.

An LSWR country station in May 1964 with passengers leaving to load their luggage into waiting cars. St. Kew Highway was an outpost of the LSWR opened in 1895 and was closed by BR on 3 October 1966.

Padstow was the end of the line as far as the LSWR was concerned and was opened on 27 March 1899. The distance to Waterloo was 260 miles and through trains were provided including the famous 'Atlantic Coast Express' which was broken into several sections as it progressed through Devon and Cornwall. T9 class No. 30709 is about to work an Okehampton train in this 1959 view. The line was closed by BR on 30 January 1967 and is now mainly a walk to Wenford known as the Camel Trail. The station at Padstow still stands.

Beattie well tank No. 30585 at Wadebridge as spare engine. The veteran 2-4-0WT was built in 1874 by Beyer Peacock for the LSWR and survived because of the light axle loading of the class which meant that they had a monopoly of the Ruthern and Wenford china clay branches. The engine can be seen today in the South Devon Railway's museum at Buckfastleigh.

On shed at Wadebridge, 21 June 1958, is veteran Beattie well tank No. 30586 of 1874 which survived until December 1962 when the three members of the class were replaced by 0-6-0 pannier tanks.

Wadebridge sees Beattie 2-4-0 well tank No. 30587 shunting in June 1958. Withdrawn in December 1962 the engine was built in 1874 and was rebuilt three times, by Adams, Urie and Maunsell. It is now preserved at Quainton Road, Buckinghamshire as SR No. E0314. The Bodmin & Wadebridge Railway was one of the oldest constituents of the Southern having been opened on 4 July 1834. The Wadebridge to Boscarne Junction section closed to all traffic on 5 September 1978.

Boscarne Junction on 5 May 1959 with 0298 class 2-4-0WT No. 30585 shunting a mixed goods. Boscarne Junction was where the GWR line from Bodmin General joined up with the LSWR from Wadebridge and Bodmin North. The present Bodmin & Wenford Railway now runs to this site.

H. F. Wheeller

Boscarne Junction on 22 June 1949 with O2 class 0-4-4T No. 206 heading for Bodmin North with a mixed train including LSWR coaches. Passenger services to Bodmin North were withdrawn on 30 January 1967.

S. C. Nash

Veteran 0298 class Beattie well tank No. 30585 takes water in Dunmere Wood from an equally ancient looking water tank. These three engines, Nos 30585-30587, long out-lasted the other members of the class as they were kept on by the Southern to work the Wenford china clay branch.

Callington was the terminus of the former Plymouth, Devonport & South Western Junction Railway which was built originally as the 3ft 6in gauge East Cornwall Mineral Railway to Calstock quay. The imposing structure of the station building included a timber roof over the platform. No. 41302, an Ivatt 2-6-2T, can be seen about to start with the Bere Alston train on 2 November 1958.

Bere Alston to Callington

The present Gunnislake line to Plymouth was once the 9½-mile Callington branch to Bere Alston and from there onwards the line was the former LSWR main line from Exeter to Plymouth. The Gunnislake branch is kept at present as it affords access from one side of the River Tamar to the other. The top end of the line, from Gunnislake to Callington, closed to all traffic on 7 November 1966. The former main line of the

LSWR from Bere Alston to Meldon closed to all traffic on 6 May 1968, the section from Bere Alston to Victoria Road (Plymouth) having been singled. The Callington line started out as the 3ft 6in gauge East Cornwall Mineral Railway which ran to Calstock Quay. The line was opened on 7 May 1872 and not extended to Bere Alston until 2 March 1908, where it joined the main line. The railway became the Plymouth, Devonport & South Western Junction Light Railway and was

The PD&SWJR had two 0-6-2 tanks in their fleet which became SR Nos 757 and 758. These were built by Hawthorn, Leslie in 1907, together with 756. No. 30758 *Lord St. Levan* is seen at Eastleigh awaiting withdrawal.

Hugh Ballantyne

182

An Ivatt 2-6-2T crosses the River Tamar at Calstock in 1963 on the former Callington line which was opened through to Bere Alston in 1907. It was closed by BR from Callington back to Calstock on 7 November 1966.

Hugh Ballantyne

Class O2 No. 30182 is about to set out for Turnchapel with an RCTS special consisting of LSWR gated push-and-pull stock. The train is seen at Plymstock where the branch diverged from the GWR Yealmpton line.

Hugh Ballantyne

Adams O2 class 0-4-4T No. 30182 arrives at Turnchapel with the RCTS special. The branch closed to passengers on 10 September 1951 and freight on 20 October 1961.

Hugh Ballantyne

converted to standard gauge throughout. The main line from Lydford to Devonport Junction was PD&SWJR but was leased to and operated as part of the LSWR main line.

Branch lines at Plymouth
The LSWR had a passenger terminal at Plymouth Friary and Southern trains to London started from here until rationalisation in the area brought about closure to passenger traffic on 15 September 1958. The present Southern Friary branch is still open for freight and the Cattewater line is open for oil trains. The Plymstock line originally went to Turnchapel, some 2½ miles from Friary was closed to passengers on 10 September 1951 and freight on 20 October 1961. The LSWR branch from Devonport Kings Road to Stonehouse Pool closed to all traffic on 30 May 1970. The old LSWR main line through Devonport to St Budeaux closed to passengers on 7 September 1964

London and South Western Ry.

——— (787)

*From*_____

TO

PLYMOUTH (FRIARY)

London and South Western Ry.

787

SEATON Jct. TO

DEVONPORT

Appendix 1

Southern Region Lines of Great Western Origin

The Southern Region included several lines which were not of Southern Railway origin. There were also lines which closed as Western Region lines but had belonged to the Southern Railway. After Nationalisation in 1948 regional boundaries changed several times, the most noticeable being the Southern Railway lines west of Exeter. In 1950 all Southern lines in that area became Western Region, but were still used by the Southern Region for operating purposes. In 1958 Southern lines west of Exeter were transferred back to the Southern Region. This situation existed until 1 January 1963 when all Southern lines west of Wilton South were transferred to the Western Region, including all surviving branch lines. For the visitor to the West of England this could be confusing as some stations were painted chocolate and cream but had green nameboards, and vice versa.

GWR lines transferred to the Southern Region were Chard to Taunton and Yeovil to Taunton, (closed to all traffic on 6 July 1964), and Yeovil to Castle Cary. Bridport (closed completely 5 May 1975), Abbotsbury (closed completely 1 December 1952), Newbury to Winchester (DNSR closed completely 10 August 1964), and Savernake to Andover Junction (closed completely 11 September 1961). The Andover Junction to Ludgershall section is still retained for military purposes. In addition, the lines from Basingstoke to Reading and from Westbury to Salisbury are of ex-GWR origin but have at some time been Southern Region.

The Somerset & Dorset Railway, jointly owned by the Southern Railway and the LMSR, became Western Region above Templecombe and Southern below. As the line originated from the Midland & LSWR prior to 1923, a wide variety of locomotive classes and rolling stock could be seen. The Somerset & Dorset was closed down completely in 1966.

Appendix 2

Light Railways Act 1896

Towards the end of the 19th century, railway promoters were having difficulty in providing new lines to remote areas, where the costs were marginal but the railway to a small community was considered essential for the development of the area. In the pre-motor age it must be remembered that the horse and cart was the only alternative to the railway for inland transport if one discounts the even slower canals. In order to serve rural areas light railways were constructed at a cheaper rate than a full main line railway. This involved lightly laid track, minimum ballasting, no crossing gates or keeper and little or no signalling. In the case of most light railways, trains were worked on the 'one engine in steam' principal. Tunnels and heavy engineering works were also usually absent on light railways, as were staff at stations – and in some cases stations themselves. The system was successful until buses and lorries started to ply upgraded roads, and when the country bus was firmly established the light railway was doomed.

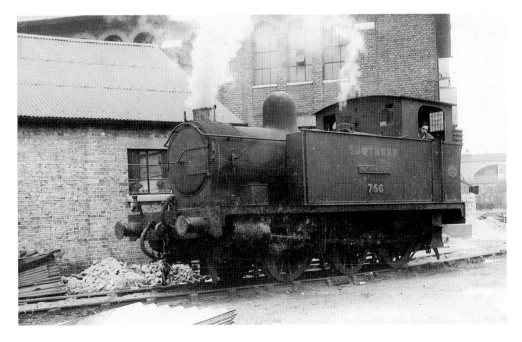

Southern Railway No. 756 *A. S. Harris* was built in 1907 by Hawthorn, Leslie for the Plymouth, Devonport & South Western Junction Railway and was the solitary example of the class. The 0-6-0T ended its days at Stewarts Lane and can be seen minus chimney shortly before withdrawal.

Bibliography

Rail Atlas Great Britain & Ireland S. K. Baker (OPC 1980 & 1996)

Passengers no more G. Daniels & L. Dench (Ian Allan 1980)

Preserved Locomotives H. C. Casserley (Ian Allan 1980)

A Guide to Steam Railways of Great Britain Rev. W. Awdry & C.Cook (Pelham 1979)

B.R. Pregrouping Atlas W. P. Conolly (Ian Allan 1958)

Branch Line Index G. C. Lewthwaite (BLS 1971)

L. & S.W.R. Locomotives 1873-1922 F. Burt (Ian Allan 1949)

Locomotive History of S.E. & C.R. D. L. Bradley (RCTS 1980)

The Elham Valley Line Brian Hart (Wild Swan 1984)

The Meon Valley Railway R. A. Stone (Kingfisher 1983)

Lines to Torrington John Nicholas (OPC 1984)

History of the Southern Railway R. W. Kidner/D. Marshall (Ian Allan 1963)

William Stroudley, Craftsman of Steam H. J. Campbell Cornwell (David & Charles 1968)

The Axminster to Lyme Regis Railway E. J. Rose (Kingfisher 1982)

The London, Chatham & Dover Railway Adrian Gray (Maresborough 1984)

Railway Magazine, Railway World, Steam World and *Branch Line News.*

Also, Oakwood Press paperbacks, various editions, and the publications by Peter Harding.

London, Chatham & Dover motive power for suburban duties came in the form of 0-4-4 tanks. No. 166 poses here at Crystal Palace (High Level) in pre-amalgamation days. The Kirtley tanks were built in 1880 by Kitson of Leeds and were classified A1 by the LCDR. The class became extinct in 1926 under the Southern but the retaining wall behind the engine survives, the site now being occupied by a housing estate.

M7 class 0-4-4T No. 30111 at Brockenhurst in June 1963. The engine has worked the push-and-pull train from Bournemouth West via Wimborne, a service that was withdrawn on 4 May 1964

J. Phillips

O2 class No. W27 *Merstone* at Ryde St Johns Road shed on the Isle of Wight, 26 June 1960. This was one of the Adams 0-4-4Ts fitted with a Drummond boiler.

Lamp post and station nameboard, photographed in February 1960. Of LBSCR origin the oil lamp would show up the station name which was inserted in the lamp case. The BR regional totem has been added to the lamp standard.

Passenger luggage labels could be found for even the most remote parts of the system. The LSWR standard white labels were available at Waterloo and were stored in a large rack in the booking hall. Every LSWR destination was available including the Basingstoke & Alton and Lynton & Barnstaple railways. The LBSCR had standard labels and always printed them with the station of origin. The SECR never headed their labels but had a complicated colour system, white being the old SER main line and its branches.

London and South Western Ry.
———
787
FROM WATERLOO TO
BENTWORTH & LASHAM

London and South Western Ry.
———
787
FROM WATERLOO TO
BRATTON
(Via BARNSTAPLE JUNCTION)

London Brighton & South Coast Railway.
Steyning to
Cranleigh

London Brighton & South Coast Railway.
Hayling Island to
Cranleigh

BARHAM

BRASTED

Index to Lines

A smoky scene at Steyning with Bulleid Pacific No. 34057 *Biggin Hill* on the 7.14pm Brighton to Horsham on 12 June 1963. The Pacific is on a filling in turn from Brighton, where it was built in 1947. The engine lasted until May 1967 and the station site is now a by-pass road.

S. C. Nash

Veteran well tank No. 30585 on duty No. 607 shunts wagons at Tresaret sidings on the Wenford branch in June 1958. The china clay line to Wenford Bridge survived until 1985 and the trackbed is now the Camel Trail footpath, but trains may run again.

Line	Date Closed to Passengers	Former Company	Page
Canterbury West – Lyminge	2.12.40	SECR	60
Caterham – Purley	–	SECR	16
Chard Jcn – Chard Central	10.9.62	LSWR	151
Chessington South – Motspur Park	–	SR	22
Chichester – Midhurst	8.7.35	LIBSC	91
Christchurch – Ringwood	30.9.35	LSWR	108
Christ's Hospital – Guildford	14.6.65	LBSC	70
Christ's Hospital – Shoreham	7.3.66	LBSC	89
Cowes – Newport – Smallbrook Jcn	21.2.66	IWCR	129
Crystal Palace – Nunhead	20.9.54	SECR	9
Deptford Wharf – New Cross Gate	–	LBSC	9
Dungeness – Lydd	4.7.37	SECR	57
Dyke – Aldrington (Dyke Jcn Halt)	1.1.39	LBSC	89
East Grinstead – Lewes	17.3.58	LBSC	64
East Grinstead – Ashurst Jcn – Tun Wells West	2.1.67	LBSC	77
East Grinstead – Three Bridges	2.1.67	LBSC	70
East Southsea – Fratton	8.8.14	LSWR/LBSC	116
Easton – Melcombe Regis	3.3.52	ECHJ	151
Epsom Downs – Sutton	–	LBSC	13
Eridge – Hailsham	14.6.65	LBSC	86
Exmouth – Sidmouth Jcn	6.3.67	LSWR	157
Farnham – Ash Jcn	4.7.37	LSWR	99
Fawley – Totton	14.2.66	SR	128
Folkestone Harbour – Folkestone Jcn	–	SECR	48
Freshwater – Newport	21.9.53	FYNR	129
Fullerton – Hurstbourne	6.7.31	LSWR	108
Gosport – Fareham	8.6.53	LSWR	116
Gravesend West St. – Farningham Road	3.8.53	SECR	28

Line	Date Closed to Passengers	Former Company	..Page
Greenwich Park – Nunhead	1.1.17	SECR	9
Hailsham – Polegate	9.9.68	LBSC	86
Halwill – Torrington	1.3.65	LSWR	172
Halwill – Wadebridge	3.10.66	LSWR	174
Hampton Court-Surbiton	–	LSWR	26
Hamworthy – Poole	1896	LSWR	149
Hawkhurst – Paddock Wood	12.6.61	SECR	32
Hayes – Elmers End	–	SECR	10
Hayling Island – Havant	4.11.63	LBSC	121
Headcorn – Robertsbridge	4.1.54	KESR	52
Horsted Keynes – Haywards Heath	28.10.63	LBSCR	70
Kemp Town – London Road	2.1.33	LBSC	91
Lee-on-Solent – Fort Brockhurst	1.1.31	LSWR	121
Lewes – Seaford	–	LBSC	64
Lewes – Uckfield	24.2.69	LBSC	86
Leysdown – Queenborough	4.12.50	SECR	42
Lyme Regis – Axminster	29.11.65	LSWR	156
Lyminge – Shorncliffe	16.6.47	SECR	60
Lyminton Pier – Lymington	–	LSWR	128
Lynton – Barnstaple	30.9.35	L&BR	166
Merton Park – Tooting	3.3.29	LBSC/LSWR	22
Necropolis – Brookwood	1.5.41	BNR	27
New Romney – Appledore	6.3.67	SECR	57
Newport – Sandown	6.2.56	IWCR	129
Padstow – Bodmin North	30.1.67	LSWR	174
Petersfield – Midhurst	7.2.55	LSWR	91
Pevensey – Polegate	15.10.67	LBSC	86
Plymouth – St. Budeaux V.R.	7.9.64	LSWR	184
Plymouth Friary – North Road	15.9.58	LSWR	184
Polegate – Hailsham	9.9.68	LBSC	86
Port Victoria – Grain	11.6.51	SECR	36
Pulborough – Midhurst	7.2.55	LBSC	91
Queenborough Pier – Queenborough	1.3.23	SECR	42
Ramsgate Harbour – Broadstairs	2.7.26	SECR	48
Ramsgate Town – Margate Sands	2.7.26	SECR	48
Salisbury – West Moors	4.5.64	LSWR	144
Sandgate – Hythe	1.4.31	SECR	60
Sandling – Hythe	3.12.51	SECR	60
Sandwich Road – Eastry	1.11.28	EKLR	52
Seaton – Seaton Jcn	7.3.66	LSWR	157
Sheerness – Sittingbourne	–	SECR	42
Shepherdswell – Wingham	1.11.48	EKLR	48
Shepperton – Strawberry Hill	–	LSWR	26
Sidmouth – Sidmouth Jcn	6.3.67	LSWR	157
Stoke Jcn Halt – Grain	4.12.61	SECR	36
Swanage – Wareham	3.1.72	LSWR	151
Tattenham Corner – Purley	–	SECR	16
Tunbridge Wells West – Eridge	8.7.85	LBSC	77
Turnchapel – Plymouth Friary	10.9.51	LSWR	184
Ventnor – Shanklin	18.4.66	IWR	129
Ventnor West – Merstone	15.9.52	IWCR	129
Wenford – Boscarne Jcn	–	LSWR	174
West Croydon – Wimbledon	2.6.97	LBSC	19
Westerham – Dunton Green	30.10.61	SECR	28
Whitstable Harbour – Canterbury West	1.1.31	SECR	46
Wimbledon – Sutton	–	SR	22
Windsor & Eton – Staines	–	LSWR	26
Woodside – Selsdon	16.5.83	SE/LBSC	13
Yeovil Town – Yeovil Jcn	3.10.66	LSWR	151

LSWR branch line engines were usually of the 0-4-4T type but the Civil Engineer kept his own engine to shunt the quarry at Meldon in Devon which supplied the Southern with ballast, and is still open today. The G6 class 0-6-0T, No. DS.3152, is seen here at Eastleigh Works in June 1950. It was previously BR No. 30272, built by the LSWR at Nine Elms in February 1898. Meldon Quarry is now the terminus of the former main line from Yeoford.

Walter Gilburt

Traditional branch line motive power for LSWR services came in the form of the Adams T1 class 0-4-4Ts. Southern No. 1, built at Nine Elms in 1894, is seen here at Eastleigh awaiting scrapping on 21 August 1949.

Walter Gilburt